Medicine and Health

AMERICAN INDIAN CONTRIBUTIONS TO THE WORLD

Medicine and Health

EMORY DEAN KEOKE

KAY MARIE PORTERFIELD

CHELSEA HOUSE
PUBLISHERS
An imprint of Infobase Publishing

Medicine and Health

Chelsea House
An imprint of Infobase Publishing
132 West 31st Street
New York NY 10001

ISBN-10: 0-8160-5396-0
ISBN-13: 978-0-8160-5396-4

Library of Congress Cataloging-in-Publication Data
Keoke, Emory Dean.
    American Indian contributions to the world. Medicine and Health / Emory Dean
Keoke and Kay Marie Porterfield.
        p. cm.
Includes bibliographical references and index.
    ISBN 0-8160-5396-0 (acid-free paper)
    1. Indians of North America—Medicine. 2. Indians of North America—Health and
hygiene. 3. Traditional medicine—North America. 4. Medicinal plants—North
America. I. Porterfield, Kay Marie. II. Title.
E98.M4.K46 2005
610'.89'97—dc22   2004004291

Text design by Erika K. Arroyo
Cover design by Cathy Rincon
Maps by Sholto Ainslie
Illustrations by Dale Dyer

Printed in the United States of America

VB FOF 10 9 8 7 6 5 4 3 2

This book is printed on acid-free paper.

For our grandchildren:
Jason Keoke, Gwendolyn Z. McPherson,
Jonathan Ward McPherson, and Matthew Geboe, Jr.;
for future generations;
and in memory of Merrill W. Bowen, Jr.

CONTENTS

AUTHORS' NOTE

At least 800 unique tribes, or bands, of Indian people lived in the Americas at the time Europeans first arrived there in 1492. A tribe is a community or group of families who share the same culture, or way of living. The things that make up a culture can range from clothing and housing styles to ways of singing or praying. They include how people make and decorate the objects they use in their daily lives. Tribal members speak the same language. Sometimes the language they speak is similar to the one that their neighbors speak. It could also be very different. A list of tribes of Indian people is located at the end of this book.

American Indians were and continue to be skilled at adapting to the places where they live. From the start the features of the land where Indian people lived and the plants and animals that they found there influenced their way of life. Their cultures were also shaped by the climate and by neighboring tribes. Tribes that lived in similar regions developed many of the same ways of doing things. For example, they used many of the same medicines and developed similar styles of art. The geographical regions where similar tribes live are called culture areas. The list of tribes at the end of the book is divided into culture areas. Maps of these culture areas are also located at the back of this book. The maps contain the names of tribes that live in these areas.

Over time tribes and their cultures change. Some of the tribes mentioned in this book existed hundreds or thousands of years ago, but they do not exist as groups today. The people themselves did not vanish. Their language changed along with their way of doing things. Sometimes they moved. Sometimes they became part of other tribes.

Other tribal groups, such as the Maya of Mesoamerica, have ancient beginnings and continue to exist today. A glossary of ancient cultures that are mentioned in this book is located on page 109. Here readers will find a short explanation of when these ancient people lived and where they lived. Maps at the end of the book show the location of these ancient peoples as well.

The cultures of the first Americans were so varied and their accomplishments were so many, that it would be impossible to write everything about them in one book or even a series of books. The authors apologize in advance for anything in this book that might offend any tribe or band of American Indians. There has been no intention to speak on behalf of any tribe or to pretend knowledge in the ways of all Indian people.

INTRODUCTION

Indian peoples have lived in the Americas for at least 15,000 years. Some scientists who study the past believe that they may have come to the Americas 40,000 years ago. The very first Americans probably came from Asia, traveling over a strip of land that emerged from the sea several times during the Ice Age. By at least 10,500 B.C. they were living in what is now Monte Verde, Chile—about 11,000 miles from where they entered the continent.

By the time of European contact in 1492, at least 75 million American Indians were living in the Western Hemisphere. Some historians believe the number to be much higher. They think that 100 million to 145 million Native people lived in the Americas by the time Christopher Columbus landed in the Americas.

Good health was necessary in order for American Indians to survive and to grow in number. They learned which plants and animals provided them with the best nutrition. They discovered how to treat injuries, such as cuts and broken bones. American Indians invented treatments for their illnesses, which included headaches, fevers, tooth decay, and stomach problems. The Indian peoples of the Americas did not experience widespread waves of infectious diseases before Europeans carried the germs that cause certain diseases to the Western Hemisphere.

The first American Indians learned what plants could be used to treat sickness by experimenting. They were careful to remember which plants worked and how much medicine was safe to give to people. They also studied which plants animals ate when they were ill. Their medicines ranged from germ killers and pain relievers to heart medicines. Older people showed younger ones how to identify plants and find where they grew. They showed them how to make medicines from plants and how to use them safely. Training to become a healer, or medicine person, took many years.

▲▼▲▼▲▼▲▼▲▼▲▼▲▼▲▼▲▼▲▼▲▼▲▼▲▼▲

WARNING
The plants that Indian people used and use as medicine contain powerful substances that act on the human body. Eating the wrong plants or too much of the right ones can cause poisoning and even death. Untrained people should **not** pick and eat wild plants.

▼▲▼▲▼▲▼▲▼▲▼▲▼▲▼▲▼▲▼▲▼▲▼▲▼▲▼

Indians throughout the Americas performed operations on people, including brain surgery and skin grafts. They used anesthetics to block feelings of pain during surgery. They used antiseptics to keep their patients from getting infections. American Indian healers knew how to set broken bones and make casts. The Indians of Mesoamerica could drill and fill decaying teeth. Throughout the Americas Indian people understood that the mind and emotions can cause some diseases and can also be used to help cure them.

Today ancient American Indian medical discoveries continue to save lives. Modern medical researchers are studying Indian medicines to find more drugs that can help cure diseases. For hundreds of years American Indians of the Northwest used the bark of the Pacific yew tree to treat internal injuries and wounds. In more recent times people of the Tsimshian tribe used it to treat cancer. In the late 1960s scientists from the National Cancer Institute discovered that a chemical in the tree's bark could shrink cancer tumors. Today it is used to treat ovarian and breast cancers. It is being studied as a treatment for other types of cancers as well.

Some Indian people, who live in what is now Argentina, tie a certain kind of frog onto wounds to help them heal. Not long ago scientists thought that these people were acting on superstition (a belief that is not rational). Then a scientist learned that two substances in the frog's skin killed many kinds of germs. This living bandage provided a continuous source of medicine to the injury. Researchers hope that these substances can be used to treat diseases that resist treatment with antibiotics that are generally in use today.

Health and Nutrition

Food provides nutrients, substances that the body needs in order to live and to protect against disease. The foods that people eat (their diet) also affects how tall they grow and how many children they will have. American Indians ate a variety of nutritious foods.

HUNTERS AND GATHERERS

American Indians who hunted game or fished and who gathered wild food plants were some of the healthiest people in the world. Scientists who study the health of ancient American Indians have learned that hunters and gatherers who lived on the coast of what is now Brazil and those who lived on the coasts of what are now Southern California and South Carolina had the best health. Hunters and gatherers who lived on the Great Plains were also very healthy. The

▲▽▲▽▲▽▲▽▲▽▲▽▲▽▲▽▲▽▲▽▲▽▲▽▲▽▲▽▲

THE TALLEST PEOPLE
Hunters and gatherers of the Great Plains were the tallest people in the world in the late 1800s. The average Plains Indian man was about 5 feet, 8 inches tall, compared to European American men, who were about 5 feet, 7 inches tall. Men who lived in Europe were about 5 feet, 5 inches tall. Height is a clue to nutritional health.

▽▲▽▲▽▲▽▲▽▲▽▲▽▲▽▲▽▲▽▲▽▲▽▲▽▲▽▲▽

researchers believe that these groups of American Indians stayed so healthy because they were well nourished.

Hunters and gatherers relied on meat to supply most of their food energy. The first Indian people who lived in the Americas hunted mammoth and mastodon as well as other mammals that are now extinct. Later American Indians hunted bison, deer, elk, antelope, and wild sheep. Sometimes they ate meat from smaller animals that they hunted, including rabbit, muskrat, raccoon, and beaver. The Inuit of the Arctic hunted the sea mammals whale and seal for their meat. Indians also hunted birds, including wild turkeys and ducks, for food. Some American Indians obtained most of their nutrition from fish and fish eggs.

Meat and fish are high in proteins, substances that build and regulate the body's cells, tissues, and organs. The meat from game ani-

The Inuit people of the Arctic coast obtained most of their food from the ocean. This picture of an Inuit fisher was taken near Nome, Alaska, between 1900 and 1930. *(Library of Congress, Prints and Photographs Division, Frank and Francis Carpenter Collection [LC-USZ62-130983])*

PHYSICAL FITNESS

Early Europeans in the Americas were astonished at the exercise levels of American Indians as well as their strength and agility.

Spanish conquistador Álvar Núñez Cabeza de Vaca, who explored the southern part of what is now the United States between 1528 and 1536, wrote that the Indians of what is now Texas could run after a deer for an entire day without tiring and that they were tall and strong. "[I]n winter they go out in early dawn to take a bath, breaking the ice with their body," he wrote.

A 16th-century Spanish conquistador wrote of the Aztec: "The people of this land are well made, rather tall than short. They are swarthy as leopards . . . skillful, robust, and tireless, and at the same time the most moderate men known."

A New England colonist named James Eaton reported that Sharp Shins, one of Iroquois chief Cornplanter's messengers, could run 90 miles in one day. This may not have been accurate; however, it shows how impressed colonists were by American Indian runners.

Modern medical researchers have found that exercise is important for preventing high blood pressure, heart disease, and diabetes.

mals is especially high in protein. Bison meat contains as much as 30 percent more protein than that from cows or chickens. Meat and many types of fish also contain fat, which provides the body with energy.

Unlike people today who mostly eat muscle meat from animals, American Indian hunters and gatherers ate many parts of game animals, including the organs. These organs included the heart, kidneys, and liver. Animal fats and organs are a good source of vitamins A and D. Both of these vitamins help the body to process protein and minerals. The body uses vitamin A to grow and repair tissue. Vitamin A helps keep the skin healthy and protects the mucous membranes,

In addition to eating muscle meat, American Indians ate organ meat of wild game animals, such as this moose. The liver, heart, kidney, and adrenal glands from these animals provide more vitamins than muscle meat does. *(LaVerne Smith/U.S. Fish and Wildlife Service)*

membranes that produce mucus and line body cavities, such as the mouth. The body needs vitamin D in order to fully absorb calcium and phosphorous, two essential minerals that are needed for healthy bones and teeth. These minerals are also needed for heart and nervous system health. (The Inuit of the Arctic obtained vitamin D from whale oil and fish oil.)

American Indians whose diet consisted mostly of meat or fish obtained many minerals and much of their vitamin C from these sources as well. The body needs vitamin C to maintain healthy teeth, gums, and bones. Vitamin C helps the body to heal wounds and resist infections. It also helps to make collagen, which holds body tissues together. Animals' adrenal glands were a rich source of vitamin C for American Indians. When hunters killed a large animal, they removed

ORGAN MEATS AND B VITAMINS

The internal organs of animals are high in vitamins B_1, B_2, B_{12}, and niacin, or B_3.

B_1 (thiamine) helps the body digest certain foods and maintains the muscles, heart, and nervous system.

B_2 (riboflavin) helps the body fight disease, form red blood cells, and maintain vision as well as helping it to digest protein.

B_{12} (cobalamin) helps to form red blood cells and helps the body to absorb calcium.

Niacin, or B_3, improves circulation and lowers cholesterol as well as helps the body process fat, sugar, and protein. Niacin is also necessary for the body to be able to absorb the minerals calcium and potassium. Potassium keeps the heart beating at a steady rhythm and helps the body to eliminate waste.

the two small fatty adrenal glands above the kidneys and cut them into small pieces to share with family members.

The Inuit of the Arctic obtained most of their vitamin C from whale skin, fish eggs, and fish and whale liver. They supplemented this with vitamin C that they obtained from eating wild plants when they could find them.

VITAMIN C

The 1937 Nobel Prize in medicine was awarded to Hungarian scientist Albert Szent-Gyorgy and British chemist Sir Walter Haworth for isolating vitamin C and discovering its nutritional properties. Szent-Gyorgy unraveled the mysteries of vitamin C by analyzing the adrenal glands of an ox. American Indians obtained vitamin C by eating the adrenal glands of animals that they hunted for thousands of years before this.

Iron is a mineral that is used by the body to build red blood cells and help the body resist disease. The muscle meat of wild game animals is higher in iron than that of cattle or pigs. Organ meat contains

American Indians ate elk. Wild game contained less fat than animals raised in feedlots today. *(Jim Leupold/U.S. Fish and Wildlife Service)*

more iron than muscle meat does. American Indian hunters also obtained iron from eating marrow, the soft center of the animal's bones.

Seeds, fruits, roots, and leaves of wild plants provided American Indians with other nutrients. These plant foods were also high in fiber. The tough parts of plants that the human body cannot digest are called fiber. This fiber is needed for good digestion. Today scientists know that fiber can reduce cholesterol, a type of fat that causes heart disease. Fiber also decreases a person's chances of getting diabetes, a disease that is caused when the body does not make enough insulin. Many scientists believe that a high-fiber diet can protect against colon cancer.

A number of the plant foods that American Indians gathered contained large amounts of vitamin C. Cranberries, blueberries, and strawberries that Indians of North America gathered were especially high in this vitamin. Eight strawberries contain 140 percent of a person's daily requirement of vitamin C.

By eating foods that contained vitamin C, American Indians avoided getting scurvy, a disease caused by a lack of this vitamin. The symptoms of scurvy are cuts and bruises that are slow to heal, tender joints, inflamed gums, loose teeth, and eventual death.

Berries provided American Indians with many more health benefits. Eating cranberries or drinking their juice can prevent kidney and bladder infections. Cranberries contain substances that prevent *Escherichia coli* (*E. coli*) bacteria from attaching to cells in the urinary tract. Blueberries contain a substance that also kills *E. coli* and other bacteria. In addition to vitamin C, blueberries contain high levels of vitamins A and E and a great deal of iron. Vitamin E is an antioxidant that protects the cells from being broken down by free radicals. Free radicals are harmful by-products of metabolism, chemical changes in the body that allow it to live and grow.

▲▽▲▽▲▽▲▽▲▽▲▽▲▽▲▽▲▽▲▽▲▽▲▽▲▽▲▽▲▽▲

A CURE FOR SCURVY

In 1536 when French explorer Jacques Cartier's ship became icebound in the frozen St. Lawrence River near the Indian village that would become Montreal, 25 of his crew members died from scurvy. The Europeans did not know how to cure this disease. A Huron leader showed the explorer how to grind the bark of an evergreen tree and prepare a tea that contained vitamin C. Within eight days the remaining sick crew members were cured. Many of the tonics that American Indians made from medicinal plants were filled with vitamins and minerals that kept them healthy by preventing disease.

▼▲▼▲▼▲▼▲▼▲▼▲▼▲▼▲▼▲▼▲▼▲▼▲▼▲▼▲▼▲▼

American Indians who gathered traditional foods maintained a high level of calcium in their diets. Calcium is a mineral that is necessary for growing and maintaining strong bones, teeth, and muscles. Calcium also contributes to nervous system health and helps regulate blood pressure. In the Southwest, American Indians ate the buds from the cholla cactus. One tablespoon of these buds contains the same amount of calcium as an eight-ounce glass of milk. Seedpods from the mesquite cactus also provided them with calcium as well as other minerals, including iron and zinc. Zinc helps to maintain skin, hair, and bones and is essential for good night vision.

▲▽▲▽▲▽▲▽▲▽▲▽▲▽▲▽▲▽▲▽▲▽▲▽▲▽▲▽▲▽▲

LACTOSE INTOLERANCE

Unlike Europeans, American Indians did not eat milk, butter, or cheese in order to obtain calcium. There were no cattle in the Americas for Indians to tame, and mountain goats could not be tamed so they had no source of dairy foods. Because of this, more than 75 percent of American Indians are lactose intolerant. This means that their bodies do not produce enough of the enzyme lactase to digest the simple sugar called lactose that is present in milk. An enzyme is a protein that triggers a chemical reaction. When lactose-intolerant people drink milk they experience stomach pain, bloating, and diarrhea. (About 15 percent of northern Europeans have lactose intolerance.)

▼▲▼▲▼▲▼▲▼▲▼▲▼▲▼▲▼▲▼▲▼▲▼▲▼▲▼▲▼▲▼

Navajo (Dineh) people burned juniper branches and ground them into powder. They used this powder in the traditional foods that they cooked. Juniper ash contained minerals that helped to build healthy bones. American Indians of other tribes ate other varieties of calcium-rich plants.

American Indians also gathered plants that provided them with iodine. Iodine is a mineral that the body needs in order to help the thyroid gland produce hormones that regulate growth and reproduction. When the body does not get enough iodine, the thyroid gland enlarges and the neck swells. This enlargement is called a goiter.

American Indians along the Pacific Coasts of North America, Mesoamerica, and South America ate iodine-rich seaweed called kelp to prevent goiter. The Inca, whose empire was established in about A.D. 1000 in what are now Peru and parts of Bolivia, dried the kelp and distributed it to people who lived far from the ocean.

Indian people who lived on both coasts of the Americas also ate fish eggs, which are high in iodine. Indians of Mesoamerica used sea salt that they made by evaporating seawater. Sea salt contains iodine.

Seaweed was an important source of iodine for the people who lived on the coasts of the Americas. This picture of Clayoquot women of the Northwest was taken near Vancouver, British Columbia, in about 1910. *(Library of Congress, Prints and Photographs Division, Edward S. Curtis Collection [LC-USZ62-115812])*

Today in the United States and Canada iodine is added to table salt in order to prevent goiters.

FARMERS

Farming Indians of North America and Mesoamerica often raised corn, beans, and squash. These three foods made up a large part of their diet. When corn and beans are eaten together, they combine to form a complete protein. Protein is made of eight essential amino acids. In order for the body to use these amino acids to grow and repair cells, they must all be present in the stomach at the same time. Squash contains high levels of vitamin C and calcium as well as other vitamins and minerals.

Most of the niacin that corn contains is bound to starch, or carbohydrates. It passes through the body without being used. Indians

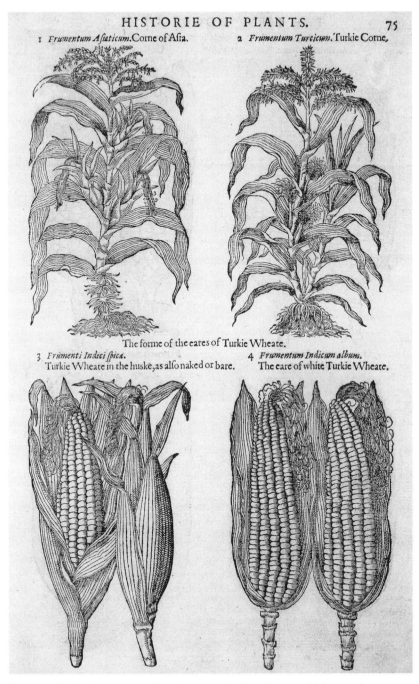

HISTORIE OF PLANTS. 75

1 *Frumentum Afiaticum.* Corne of Afia. 2 *Frumentum Turcicum.* Turkie Corne.

The forme of the eares of Turkie Wheate.

3 *Frumenti Indici fpica.*
Turkie Wheate in the huske, as alfo naked or bare.

4 *Frumentum Indicum album.*
The eare of white Turkie Wheate.

American Indian farmers developed many varieties of corn, which served as an important part of their diet. This drawing was published in England in John Gerard's *Herbal* in 1597. An herbal is a book of plant medicines. Europeans believed that many of the foods raised by the Indians of the Americas were medicines. *(Library of Congress, Prints and Photographs Division [LC-USZ62-060475])*

▲▽▲▽▲▽▲▽▲▽▲▽▲▽▲▽▲▽▲▽▲▽▲▽▲▽▲▽

FARMING AND TOOTH DECAY

American Indians who farmed tended to have more cavities in their teeth than hunters and gatherers did. Many food crops contain high amounts of starch and simple sugars. Starch and sugars (carbohydrates) provide the body with energy. They also promote the growth of microorganisms that cause tooth decay. Those who ate very little meat also sometimes did not obtain enough iron.

▽▲▽▲▽▲▽▲▽▲▽▲▽▲▽▲▽▲▽▲▽▲▽▲▽▲▽

of the Americas discovered a way to solve this problem. Mesoamerican cooks and those who lived in the Southwest soaked dry kernels in lime water. Lime, or calcium carbonate, also added calcium to their diet. Other Indian cooks of North America soaked dried corn in a combination of water and wood ash. This way of soaking corn made it easier for the body to absorb the niacin contained in corn. Corn that has been soaked in wood ash or lime water has fewer sugars than unprocessed corn does. The starches that it contains are digested slowly, keeping blood sugar levels stable.

Corn that has been processed in lime or wood ash water is called hominy. Today it continues to be an important ingredient in Mexican food. Flour made from hominy is called *masa*. Masa harina, finely ground meal that is made in factories, is used for making tamales, tortillas, and tortilla chips today.

When Europeans began eating corn, they did not understand that they needed to process it. Those who ate large amounts of corn developed a disease called *pellagra* that is caused by niacin (vitamin B_3) deficiency. The symptoms of pellagra include skin rashes and blisters, nausea, diarrhea, and thinking difficulties. By the 1900s many people in Europe, Africa, and the United States were dying

▲▽▲▽▲▽▲▽▲▽▲▽▲▽▲▽▲▽▲▽▲▽▲▽▲▽▲▽

HIGH PROTEIN CORN

American Indians of the Southwest ate blue corn. Blue corn has a higher level of lysine, an essential amino acid, than do other types of corn. Blue corn also has 30 percent more protein than yellow dent corn, the type of corn that is most often raised for human food today.

▽▲▽▲▽▲▽▲▽▲▽▲▽▲▽▲▽▲▽▲▽▲▽▲▽▲▽

from this disease. In 1914 scientists learned how to prevent pellagra—something American Indians had known for thousands of years.

AMERICAN INDIAN "SUPERFOODS"

A number of the crops that American Indian farmers planted and harvested are considered "superfoods" today because of their high nutritional content. Some of these foods contain phytochemicals. Phytochemicals are chemical compounds that prevent disease. Some phytochemicals are used to treat disease.

Amaranth

Amaranth is a plant with high-protein seeds that Mesoamerican farmers raised. Amaranth seeds have as much of the amino acid lysine as is found in cow's milk. This makes amaranth's protein more complete than that of many other plants. Amaranth seeds are a good source of vitamin E and the B vitamins. They are also high in the minerals calcium, potassium, iron, magnesium, and zinc. Magnesium maintains the heart's rhythm and helps convert blood sugar into energy.

Blue-Green Algae

Blue-green algae are tiny plants that grow in water and have no leaves, stems, or roots. These plants, which are also called spirulina, are 70 percent protein. When algae is combined with corn it creates a complete protein. Blue-green algae contains many vitamins. The Aztec, who established an empire in Mesoamerica starting in about A.D. 1100, harvested algae from lakes and dried it. They used it in tortillas and for making sauces.

Chia

Chia is a desert plant that produces seeds that contain saponins. Saponins are phytochemicals that lower cholesterol and may slow the growth of cancer cells. (Cholesterol is a fatlike substance that is produced by the liver. It helps the body to metabolize food. Too much cholesterol can clog the arteries and cause heart attacks.) American Indians ate chia seeds when they had to travel long distances without food or water. Yams and beans are other American Indian foods that contain saponins.

Chilies

Chilies were first domesticated by Indian farmers of Mesoamerica. They contain twice the amount of vitamin C as is found in citrus fruits. Chilies contain high amounts of vitamins A, B_1, and E. They also contain lycopene, an antioxidant. Many researchers believe that lycopene may prevent some kinds of cancer and heart disease.

Quinoa

Quinoa is a seed-producing plant grown by farmers who lived in the Andes Mountains of South America. Quinoa seeds are high in complete protein. Quinoa has more calcium, fat, iron, phosphorus, and B vitamins than many other grains do.

Sunflower and Pumpkin Seeds

Sunflower and pumpkin seeds have high iodine content. American Indians living inland, far from the seacoast, prevented goiter by eating them. These seeds are high in healthful unsaturated fats (fats that are liquid at room temperature). They also contain large amounts of vitamin E and folate, a B complex vitamin that helps cells to grow. They also contain zinc, which has been shown to protect against disease by boosting the body's immune system.

Tomatoes

Tomatoes contain high amounts of lycopene. According to a recent study, people who ate seven or more servings of tomatoes a week reduced their chances of developing colon or rectal cancer by 69 percent. One medium tomato provides 40 percent of the daily vitamin C requirement for an adult.

CHANGES IN AMERICAN INDIAN DIETS

Soon after 1492 Europeans began taking the land where Indian people hunted and gathered food as well as the land on which they raised crops. Conquistadores and colonists began exporting crops that American Indians had raised to Europe, Asia, and Africa. As a result, the nutritional content of the diet of people throughout the world improved. Today three out of every four food crops raised throughout the world were once raised by American Indians.

At the same time that American Indian foods were introduced throughout the world, American Indians were suddenly expected to eat the foods that non-Indians did. In North America, Indian people who signed treaties obtained food rations from the U.S. government and the Dominion of Canada in exchange for their land. In the

TOBACCO
A Modern Health Problem

Tobacco plants grew in the Americas for thousands of years. American Indians living on the coast of Brazil first began planting and harvesting tobacco in about A.D. 1. From there, tobacco farming spread throughout North America, Mesoamerica, and South America. Indian people used tobacco as medicine. Some tribes used tobacco leaves as dressing for wounds. Others used them as a toothache remedy. American Indians also smoked tobacco as part of religious ceremonies or social gatherings such as meetings between leaders.

The dangers of casual tobacco use were something many of American Indians understood. For example, the Akimel O'odham (Pima) and Tohono O'odham (Papago) of the North American desert Southwest grew tobacco, but only old men and old women smoked it because they believed that smoking made young men cough and drained their energy.

After Europeans first saw tobacco, they also used it as a medicine. Europeans soon developed a smoking habit. This habit spread quickly. As tobacco use increased in Europe, the crop became more profitable for European traders and colonial farmers than gold.

In modern times widespread recreational smoking has become one of the leading medical problems throughout the world. Since many American Indians began using tobacco as non-Indians did, tobacco use has become a major health problem for them as well.

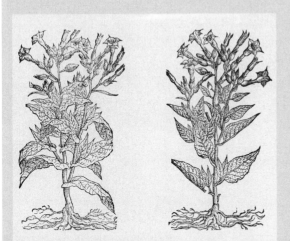

American Indians smoked tobacco mainly in ceremonies. For Europeans smoking soon became a harmful habit. Today tobacco use is responsible for 30 percent of all cancer deaths. This drawing of a tobacco plant from the Caribbean was printed in the 1633 edition of Gerard's *Herbal*. (Courtesy of the National Library of Medicine)

United States these rations included corn and corn meal that had not been soaked in wood ash or lime. As a result some Indian people developed pellagra.

Many of the foods that American Indians were given to eat, such as wheat flour and refined sugar, were low in fiber and high in starch and sugars. These foods cause tooth decay. They are also digested more rapidly than traditional American Indian foods and raise the level of sugar in the blood. This makes the body's insulin ineffective and can eventually cause type II, or adult onset, diabetes. American Indians in the United States were encouraged to raise cows and drink the milk they produced in order to obtain their calcium. Most Indian people could not drink milk. European-American farmers believed that many of the plants that American Indian people once gathered for food were weeds. They plowed them under and later began spraying them with chemical herbicides, or weed killers, that made them unsafe to eat.

Today American Indians have many illnesses caused by changes in diet and lifestyle. These illnesses include heart disease, high blood pressure, obesity, and diabetes. To reverse this trend, many health-conscious American Indian people are now returning to the foods that kept their ancestors healthy for thousands of years. Many have also stopped smoking.

Personal Hygiene

2

Indian people throughout the Americas practiced personal hygiene habits that kept them healthy and prevented disease. Whenever possible, they bathed daily. They took steps to care for their skin and hair. They also discovered how to control insects. Indians of North America were careful to dispose of human waste away from their encampments or villages. Indians of Mesoamerica and South America developed more formal practices to keep their cities clean.

BATHING

American Indians viewed bathing as a way to prevent illness and as a way to treat it. Indians of many tribes also believed that bathing was a form of purifying oneself spiritually. Indian people bathed in lakes, streams, and rivers.

They also took baths in natural hot springs. The Maya of Mesoamerica bathed in hot springs. Maya culture flourished in Mesoamerica beginning in about 1500 B.C. Montezuma (Moctezuma),

---

HOT SPRINGS

Hot springs are created when water seeps close to molten, or melted, rock beneath the surface of the Earth. Molten rock is very hot—about 1,000 to 1,200 degrees centigrade, or 1,832 to 2,192 degrees Fahrenheit. The heated water rises and returns to the surface of the Earth through cracks in the Earth's crust. As it rises, it cools.

the Aztec emperor when the Spaniards arrived in what is now Mexico in 1519, built one of his large gardens around a hot spring, so that he could bathe surrounded by fragrant flowers.

American Indians at one time used all of the known hot springs in the United States and Canada. In the United States alone, there are more than 115 large hot springs and at least 1,800 smaller ones. The Iroquois people bathed at Saratoga Springs in what is now New York State, stopping there during hunting trips. Indians of California used the hot mud from springs at what is now Calistoga, California, to treat muscle and joint aches. They built wooden houses over some of the smaller springs in order to trap the steam. They used these houses like saunas.

American Indians visited what is now Hot Springs National Park, in central Arkansas, to bathe, starting about 10,000 years ago. They believed that the hot water bubbling from the earth was a gift from the Creator. Indian people declared the spring neutral ground where no arguments could take place. Spanish explorer Hernando de Soto is thought to be the first European to have seen this spring in 1541.

After colonists staked claim to the hot springs throughout the continent, they turned them into health resorts. The Minnekata Hotel in Hot Springs, South Dakota, was located about 50 miles from Wounded Knee, which is on the Pine Ridge Reservation. This picture was taken in 1889, one year before the Wounded Knee Massacre, when the U.S. Army killed the Lakota leader Big Foot and more than 300 members of his band, including women, children, and the elderly. *(Library of Congress, Prints and Photographs Division [LC-USZ62-4404])*

The sweat lodges of the Navajo (Dineh) people resembled the earliest houses, or hogans, that they built in the Southwest. *(Library of Congress, Prints and Photographs Division [LC-USZ62-80365])*

Some historians believe that the Fountain of Youth that de Soto and Juan Ponce de León looked for was actually a hot spring.

Indians throughout the Americas also bathed in steam rooms, or sweat baths. To make steam, North American Indian bathers poured water over rocks that they had heated in a fire. To provide privacy and to keep the steam in one area, American Indians built small enclosures that were used only for bathing. Indians of the Plains built sweat lodges from sapling frames that they covered with hides. People of the Southwest built their steam rooms from earth mounded over log frames. The Maya and Aztec people of Mesoamerica made steam baths from rock. In Aztec cities, most homes or clusters of homes had a sweat bath. Sweathouses were used throughout the Americas for healing ceremonies as well as for bathing.

▲▽▲▽▲▽▲▽▲▽▲▽▲▽▲▽▲▽▲▽▲▽▲▽▲▽▲

A SHOCKING HABIT

Andrés de Tapia, a conquistador who accompanied Hernán Cortés in what is now Mexico recorded that Montezuma "washed his body twice a day." In Peru the Spaniards who accompanied Francisco Pizarro were astonished at the bathing habits of the Inca. The Inca, who established an empire in what is now Peru in about A.D. 1000, used copper pipes to transport hot and cold water to the sunken bathtubs in their bathhouses. These tubs had spouts, drains, and shelves for bathing supplies.

Such attention to bathing shocked the conquistadores. In Europe people rarely bathed because the Roman Catholic Church forbade it. Queen Isabella of Spain, who funded the voyages of Christopher Columbus, is said to have taken only two baths in her entire life.

▽▲▽▲▽▲▽▲▽▲▽▲▽▲▽▲▽▲▽▲▽▲▽▲▽▲▽

In order to cleanse their skin, hair, and clothing, American Indians used plant-based detergents. A detergent is a substance made up of long, thin molecules. The end of a detergent molecule, which is called the head, is attracted to water. The other end of the detergent molecule, which is called the tail, is repelled by water and attracted to grease and dirt. Detergent molecules break oil into droplets. With their heads facing out, they surround drops of oil and specks of dirt to form tiny clumps called micelles. The clumps combine with the water and can be easily rinsed away. Unlike soap, which is made from animal or vegetable fat, detergents lather in hard water (water that contains high levels of minerals). Detergents do not leave scum as soap does.

Wherever they lived, American Indians found plants containing saponin, a substance that acts as a detergent. They used these plants to wash their clothing as well as themselves. The Karok, a California tribe, mashed the bulbs of the soap plant, which they used to clean their clothing and buckskin blankets. Buckskin is animal skin that has been tanned to keep it soft. Karok people also rubbed the roots and crushed leaves of saltbrush on their clothing to clean it. California tribes used whole soap-plant bulbs when they bathed, much as people use bars of soap or detergent today. They used these plants as shampoos as well.

The people of Southern California tribes used wild gourd, or buffalo gourd, as laundry detergent and bleach. They used both the root and the mashed pulp and seeds of this plant. The Tohono O'odham (Papago), who lived in the desert of what is now Arizona, washed clothing with wild gourd. Pueblo people of the Southwest sometimes cut the gourds in half and rubbed them on their clothing as a prewash stain remover.

American Indians who lived in the Southwest and in the Great Basin area used roots from yucca plants for detergent. They roasted the roots of these plants in order to release the saponin from them. They used yucca as a body wash and shampoo as well as for cleaning their clothing. In the Southeast, the Cherokee made detergent from bear grass roots, a variety of yucca. Yucca cleans so well that several shampoos sold today contain yucca.

The Aztec used many plants as detergents. One of these was a tree that they called *copalxocatl.* Spaniards later called this the soap tree. The *copalxocatl* produced small fruits that contained a chemical that produced lather when it was mixed with water. The Aztec also used the roots of two plants that contain saponin. They crushed these roots before adding them to water.

▲▽▲▽▲▽▲▽▲▽▲▽▲▽▲▽▲▽▲▽▲▽▲▽▲▽▲▽▲

CLOTHING FRESHENER

Today people place scented sheets of fabric softener into the dryer to give their laundry a pleasant scent. Indians who lived on the Great Plains often stored dried sweetgrass with their buckskin clothing in order to make it smell fresh.

▽▲▽▲▽▲▽▲▽▲▽▲▽▲▽▲▽▲▽▲▽▲▽▲▽▲▽▲▽

HAIR CONDITIONERS

After American Indians had washed their hair with detergents, they used conditioners to add shine and make their hair easier to manage. The Aztec boiled sunflower seeds to release the oil. They used the oil as a rinse, much like a modern hot oil hair treatment.

North American Indian people of many tribes used purified animal fat as a hair conditioner. To purify the fat, they heated it and skimmed impurities from the surface. Then they added herbs to provide fragrance. For example, the Omaha, who lived on the southern

▲▽▲▽▲▽▲▽▲▽▲▽▲▽▲▽▲▽▲▽▲▽▲▽▲▽▲▽▲▽▲

ANCIENT DEODORANT

The Aztec used several sweet-smelling plant substances as underarm deodorants and as perfume. These included American balsam oil, copal gum, and liquid amber. Copal gum is the sweet smelling sap from copal trees that grow in the Mesoamerican lowlands. *Copalli* is a Nahuatl (Aztec) word that means "resin." Liquid amber is the golden brown resin that the sweetgum tree produces when its branches are cut. American Indian people of what is now southern Mexico traded liquid amber to the Aztec, who used it for incense as well as deodorant.

▽▲▽▲▽▲▽▲▽▲▽▲▽▲▽▲▽▲▽▲▽▲▽▲▽▲▽▲▽▲▽

Great Plains, added prairie rose petals and wild bergamot. The Blackfeet and the Kootenai of the northern plateau used needles of the balsam fir. The Chippewa (Anishinabe) of the Great Lakes used balsam gum as an ingredient. Balsam is an ingredient in modern hair conditioners and shampoos.

American Indians living in what are now southern Arizona, California, and Baja California rinsed their hair with conditioners made from jojoba seeds. They also used jojoba seeds as a skin conditioner. Jojoba is a desert shrub. The seeds of this plant contain a substance that acts like an oil but is a liquid wax. Unlike oils, liquid waxes do not break down under heat and pressure. They stay fresh for a long time and have no odor. Today jojoba is used in shampoos, conditioners, soaps, sunscreen, and as a base for body lotions and moisturizing creams.

SKIN CARE

To protect their skin from cold weather, wind, and sun, American Indians used many types of skin lotions and salves. American Indians also used jojoba as a skin conditioner. In the 1700s Father Junípero Serra, founder of 21 California missions, wrote in his diary that Indians used jojoba as a salve for bruises, sores, cuts, and burns. The Zuni, who continue to live in what is now New Mexico, used the western wallflower as a sun-

American Indians of the Southwest made wallflower into a sunburn lotion.
(Gary M. Stoltz/U.S. Fish and Wildlife Service)

A medicine bundle hangs outside of this Cheyenne cabin near Lame Deer, Montana, in 1941. In addition to sacred objects, medicine bundles contained dried plants that were used as medicines. To heal sores on the skin, the Cheyenne made a salve from ponderosa pine sap. *(Library of Congress, Prints and Photographs Division [LC-USF34-058283-D])*

screen. They ground the wallflower and mixed it with water. They then applied it to their skin to prevent sunburn. They also used wallflower as a treatment for sunburn.

American Indians of the Southwest also treated sunburn with the gel of the agave, a cactus. Today agave gel is used in skin lotions and as a skin-softening ingredient in some soaps.

In other parts of North America, Indians used fats from animals, such as bear, as skin softeners. They also used oil from fish or plants. Northeastern tribes used oil that they made from sunflower seeds that they had grown. The Iroquois of the Northeast made hand lotion by boiling the juice from cornstalks. They used dried cornstalks as a container for this hand lotion. American Indians who lived near petroleum deposits in what is now Pennsylvania rubbed oil on their skin to protect it.

INSECT CONTROL

Lice are tiny insects that are generally found in the outdoors. These insects are parasites that feed on animal and human blood. Parasites are animals or plants that feed on other animals or plants without killing them or benefiting them. Once lice have found a human being to live on, they make their home on the hair-covered parts of the body and reproduce there. Today, these parasites are known to spread disease. American Indians developed several plant remedies to combat lice before contact with Europeans.

For example, the Paiute and Shoshone people of the Great Basin washed their hair in a hot mixture of sweetroot and water. The Bella

BARBERS

Long before contact with Europeans, the Aztec people had invented barbershops. Aztec men went to barbershops to have their heads shaved or their hair trimmed or washed. Sometimes the men of Mesoamerica removed facial hair with tweezers. In addition to being fashionable, these practices were practical because they discouraged insects.

Sometimes, instead of shaving, men of what is now Peru plucked their facial hair out using tweezers. Later, the Inca and also the Aztec of Mesoamerica used tweezers as medical instruments as well. The man on this pot, which was probably made in about A.D. 650, is shown plucking his facial hair with tweezers. (Neg. No. 21A3458; Courtesy Department of Library Services, American Museum of Natural History)

Coola people of what is now British Columbia rubbed mashed mountain ash berries onto their scalps. The Tsimshian people, who lived in the same region, used mashed devil's club berries. The West Coast Karok used a preparation they made from the roots of the gum plant.

Conquistadores and colonists generally believed that Indian people were unclean even though Indians bathed more frequently than the newcomers did. Many settlers also thought that all Indian people had lice and that having lice did not bother them. The European Americans were convinced that these beliefs were proof that American Indians were more animal than human. In truth, lice had been a daily fact of life in Europe for centuries. From the 1400s through the American frontier period in the mid-1800s, Indians, conquistadores, and colonists alike, often had lice.

American Indians found ways to repel other types of insects as well. The Salish, who lived on the West Coast, rubbed wild onion bulbs on the skin. The Cherokee, a tribe of the Southeast, pounded the root of the herb goldenseal into small pieces. They mixed this powder with bear fat and rubbed it on their bodies to discourage insects. The Iroquois mixed chestnut oil with bear grease to make an insect repellent.

Just as American Indians wanted their bodies free of insects, they wanted their homes and belongings to be free of insects as well. Throughout the Americas, Indian people burned dried plants to discourage mosquitoes and flies. In North America, the Kootenai people of the Plateau Region sprinkled crushed, dried mint leaves on their belongings to keep them insect free. Other tribes did this as well.

In the North American Southwest, the Anasazi and later the Pueblo people kept their homes free from insects with buffalo gourd, the same plant that they used as a detergent. In addition to saponins, buffalo gourd contains bitter chemicals that are called cucurbitacins

▽▲▽▲▽▲▽▲▽▲▽▲▽▲▽▲▽▲▽▲▽▲▽▲▽▲▽▲▽▲

INSECT BITE REMEDIES

American Indians had a number of remedies to ease the discomfort caused by insect bites. The Inupiaq people, who lived in the northwest part of what is now Canada, placed mashed willow leaves on bites to take away the pain and swelling. Willow contains salicin, the active ingredient in aspirin. The Maya put papaya leaves on insect bites. Papaya leaves contain papain, a substance that breaks down the protein in meat. Modern scientists think that papain may do the same with insect venom.

▽▲▽▲▽▲▽▲▽▲▽▲▽▲▽▲▽▲▽▲▽▲▽▲▽▲▽▲▽▲▽

Pueblo people relied on the buffalo gourd to keep insects away from their homes. This man and woman lived in Laguna Pueblo in New Mexico. *(Photograph No. NWDNS-111-SC-85752/National Archives and Records Administration—College Park)*

that insects avoid. Pueblo people dried the leaves and gourds. They hung them in the corners of their homes to keep insects away. They also used ground buffalo gourd roots to discourage bugs from living in their bedding.

The Maya of Mesoamerica layered the cotton material that they wove with strong-smelling plants when they stored it. They used this method to preserve documents that they wrote on amate paper, a paper made from plant fibers. The Maya also stored chili peppers with herbs to keep them free from attack by the chili moth.

The warm, wet weather of the tropics of South America provided a climate where insects flourished. People who lived in the Amazon Basin built their homes from cashew wood, which contains natural oil that repels termites. Sometimes they extracted the oil from the trees and painted it on other types of wood as an insect-repelling varnish.

SANITATION AND PLUMBING

North American Indians relied on lakes, rivers, and streams as their source of drinking water. For the most part they were careful to keep the water clean by bathing downstream

COLONIAL SANITATION

European colonists who lived in North American towns relieved themselves into chamber pots that they emptied in the streets. They also had outhouses. Often these were constructed dangerously close to drinking wells. Even large cities lacked plumbing. Boston, one of the first cities to provide water for its citizens, did so in the mid-1800s and made pipes out of wood.

from where they removed their drinking water. Indian people were also careful to use the restroom away from camp.

The Olmec, whose culture arose in the Yucatán Peninsula of what is now Mexico in about 1700 B.C., were the first known American Indians to develop plumbing. They made their water conduits of carved U-shaped blocks about three to five feet long. They covered them with capstones to keep the water from evaporating or becoming polluted. These water conduits were built to provide water to individual buildings in a community.

The Aztec of Mesoamerica built canals to bring fresh drinking water into their cities. They built other canals that were used to carry human waste away from the city. Many Aztec homes had personal restrooms. The Aztec built public restrooms as well.

▲▽▲▽▲▽▲▽▲▽▲▽▲▽▲▽▲▽▲▽▲▽▲▽▲▽▲▽▲▽

STREET SWEEPERS

The Aztec made not only personal hygiene a high priority but community cleanliness as well. Empire administrators employed street cleaners to keep the streets and walkways spotless. After they had swept the streets, they washed them to keep the dust down. Spanish conquistadores were extremely impressed by the cleanliness of Aztec cities compared to the cities of Europe.

▽▲▽▲▽▲▽▲▽▲▽▲▽▲▽▲▽▲▽▲▽▲▽▲▽▲▽▲▽▲▽

South American Indians also developed plumbing. The Chavin, whose culture flourished in what is now Peru from about 900 B.C. to 200 B.C., had plumbing, as did the Inca. Water for drinking and bathing was supplied to cities by a complex system of reservoirs, canals, and pipes. The Inca also had restrooms.

3

Disease and Disease Prevention

The most frequent medical problems that American Indians had before contact with Europeans were muscle sprains, broken bones, and wounds. American Indians who had open wounds sometimes had infections that were caused by bacteria. Bacteria are single-celled organisms that multiply in the body and can make people sick by producing toxins, or poisons.

American Indians suffered from tooth decay. Elderly American Indians often had joint pain from arthritis or rheumatism. Sometimes Indian women experienced difficulty in childbirth. Headaches, fevers, and coughs as well as eye irritations were part of American Indian life. Occasionally American Indian people had stomachaches and other digestion problems after eating food that did not agree with them or food that had spoiled.

A HEALTHY ENVIRONMENT

American Indians had fewer domesticated animals than Europeans did. This helped to keep them free from epidemics before European contact. Many European diseases were spread to humans from domesticated animals, such as cattle, pigs, and sheep. Some northern Europeans did not keep farm animals such as cattle and pigs in barns. They kept them in their homes as a source of heat in the winter. As a result of this close contact, diseases easily passed from animals to humans.

Intestinal worms were a common health problem for American Indians. (They were for the people throughout the world, including Europe.) These parasites live in an infected animal's or human being's intestines where they lay eggs. These eggs are excreted with the animal's or human's feces. When others touch soil or eat food contaminated with worm eggs, they can get intestinal worms. People get hookworms by walking barefoot on soil that contains hookworm larvae. (Larvae are immature hookworms that have hatched from their eggs.) Intestinal worms live on the food an animal or person eats. People with intestinal worms become pale, tired, and, weak.

Before contact with Europeans, American Indians did not experience epidemic diseases. An epidemic is a contagious disease that affects a large number of people over a wide area. A contagious disease is one that is passed from an infected animal or person to healthy animals or people. Recently scientists have found that tuberculosis (TB) existed in the precontact Americas, but that it was not widespread. Tuberculosis is a disease of the lungs that is caused by bacteria.

Indian doctors throughout the Americas developed medical treatments for all of the common health problems that precontact American Indians experienced. Many of these treatments were based on medicines made from plants that grew where Indian people lived. Others involved surgery.

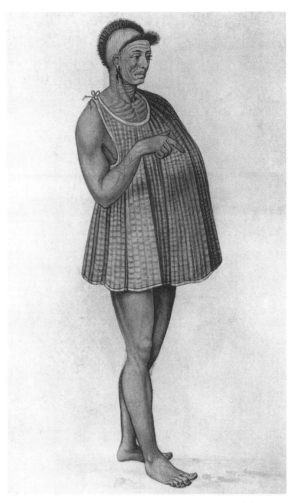

American Indian healers were often considered spiritual leaders. This copy of a drawing by John White shows an American Indian religious leader who lived near the English colonies in Virginia between 1585 and 1590. *(United States Museum/Library of Congress, Prints and Photographs Division [LC-USZ62-00588])*

Often American Indian medicine was more effective than that of Europeans at the time of contact. Spanish conquistadores wrote that they preferred to be treated by Aztec physicians rather than the Spanish doctors who traveled with them. Early North American colonists wrote that Indian people were more skilled at setting broken bones than their own doctors were. They also noted that many colonial women died from infection after giving birth, but few American

This old map of Virginia was engraved in 1624 and is based on descriptions of the area made by Captain John Smith. It shows images and locations for the Indian tribes living there. *(Library of Congress, Prints and Photographs Division [LC-USZ62-116706])*

Indian women did. Colonists were frustrated by the fact that few Indians died from infected wounds compared to colonial soldiers, who often died from infections.

STUDYING AMERICAN INDIAN HEALTH AND DISEASE

Scientists have several ways of learning about the diseases that American Indians had before contact. One way is to study the bones of human beings who have died. This study is called *paleopathology*. Examining bones provides clues about diseases that affect the

▲▼▲▼▲▼▲▼▲▼▲▼▲▼▲▼▲▼▲▼▲▼▲▼▲▼▲▼▲▼▲

THE ETHICS OF STUDYING HUMAN REMAINS

Many American Indians believe that the scientific study of human remains is a form of grave robbing. They argue that scientists would not be willing to dig up and examine bones of the scientists' own ancestors. Some scientists say that, because bones contain information about how people lived in the past, scientists have a right to study them.

In 1990 the U.S. Congress passed a law called the Native American Graves Protection and Repatriation Act. This law requires the U.S. government and museums that receive money from the U.S. government to return the American Indian human remains that they have to the Indian tribes to which the remains belong. This law also applies to American Indian human remains found on federal land, such as national parks and forests. Laws that vary from state to state cover American Indian human remains that are found off federal land.

▼▲▼▲▼▲▼▲▼▲▼▲▼▲▼▲▼▲▼▲▼▲▼▲▼▲▼▲▼▲▼

bones. Scientists have been able to tell that some groups of ancient American Indians who lived primarily on corn had anemia by looking at their bones. Anemia is a condition caused by a lack of iron in the diet. When a person does not take in enough iron over a long period of time, his or her skull bones become perforated with tiny holes.

Ancient art provides other clues about the diseases of precontact American Indians. Indians of Mesoamerica and what is now Peru in South America made pottery in the shape of human figures. The Moche people, who lived in what is now Peru from about 200 B.C. to about A.D. 600, made pottery showing people who had their feet amputated, or removed. This art provides evidence that Moche doctors were skillful at amputating feet.

Scientists also study the plant medicines that Indian healers invented. Simple coughs and fevers do not affect the skeletal system. Scientists are fairly certain that American Indians had coughs and fevers because people of many tribes developed cough medicines and medicines that lowered the body's temperature.

Scientists who study the past think that intestinal parasites were common in the precontact Americas because American Indians had many remedies for them. Indian people of the Northeast and Southeast used a two-step treatment to rid themselves of intestinal parasites. First they took plant medicine such as pinkroot for several days to kill the parasites. After that they used a laxative to expel the worms.

Europeans who came to the Americas collected information about American Indian medicine. Juan Badianus made the first written record of Aztec plant medicines. He was a Mesoamerican Indian from Xochimilco in what had then become New Spain. King Philip II of Spain was so interested in Aztec medicine that he sent his personal physician Francisco Hernández to study it in 1570. From 1571 to 1577 Hernández collected information on the plant remedies and other treatments that Aztec doctors used to cure illnesses.

The Catholic priests who traveled with the Spanish conquistadores also gathered information about medicine in Mesoamerica and the North American Southwest. The Spanish priest Bernardo de Sahagún interviewed the sons of Aztec nobility and asked them to write and draw what they knew about how Aztec physicians treated illnesses. Sahagún included that information in a book that is known today as the Florentine Codex.

North American colonists adopted many American Indian herbal medicines, too. Many of these plants, their method of preparation, and the dosage that patients were to be given were used in mainstream medicine until the 1900s.

Meriwether Lewis met with Benjamin Rush, the most famous physician in the United States, before setting out in 1804 on his journey across the North American continent with William Clark. The two leaders and their party were charged with surveying the lands of

This picture of a Great Plains medicine lodge was drawn for *Harper's Weekly Magazine* in 1868. In damp weather Indian people hung plants that were used for medicine on tipi poles to dry them. *(Courtesy of the National Library of Medicine)*

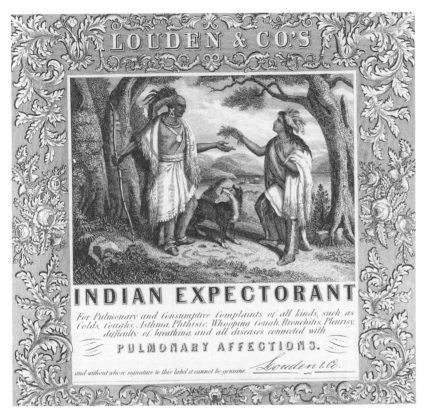

Louden's Indian Expectorant was sold in 1848. It was a cough syrup. Medicine companies that had nothing to do with Indians often put pictures of Indian people on their bottles. Because many non-Indians trusted Indian healers more than their own doctors, pictures of Indians boosted sales of these remedies. *(Library of Congress, Prints and Photographs Division [LC-USZ62-047347])*

Louisiana Purchase and finding a northwest passage to the sea. Rush gave Lewis suggestions about how to meet the medical needs of the company of explorers. Rush also gave him a list of questions about disease and medical treatment to ask when meeting with Indian tribes as he traveled across the continent.

DISEASE CONTROL

American Indians had a working knowledge that infections could be passed from person to person. In order to keep infection and disease from spreading, they separated people who were sick from those who were well. At the time of contact, most Europeans did not understand the concept of germs. Europeans first saw American Indians isolating patients with contagious diseases (those passed by contact with an infected person) among the Huron of the Northeast.

A French priest, Father Gabriel Sagard, who lived among the Huron, wrote in the 1700s, "Sometimes the medicine-man orders one of the sick people to leave the town and encamp in the woods or in some other place apart . . . usually this is only done for those who are infected with some unclean or dangerous disease, and such persons only, and no others, do they force to isolate themselves from the community until they are completely cured. This is a . . . most excellent custom and ordinance, which indeed ought to be adopted in every country."

The Continental army adopted the American Indian practice of isolating people with infections during the Revolutionary War, which began in 1775. The colonists lost more soldiers to disease than to any other cause. Fevers, pneumonia, and dysentery raged through overcrowded and often dirty military hospitals. Pneumonia is an infection of the lungs. Dysentery is an infection of the large intestine that is caused by a microorganism in contaminated drinking water. Its symptoms include bloody diarrhea, stomach cramps, and fever. Soldiers with infected wounds often developed gangrene, the death of tissue caused by loss of blood flow. Gangrene usually occurs in the hands, arms, feet, and legs. To stop the gangrene from spreading, doctors amputated soldiers' limbs.

In winter 1778 in Morristown, New Jersey, James Tilton, a Revolutionary War doctor, ordered soldiers to build small hospitals based on the floor plan of the wigwams that served as homes to Indian people of the Northeast. These log hospitals were built with a fire in the middle of the ward with a smoke hole above it for ventilation. The floors of these hospitals were earth. Patients were spaced apart with their feet toward the fire and their heads toward the walls of the building. Easing the crowding and improving ventilation helped slow the spread of disease among the troops.

American Indians also stopped infections from spreading with plants that contained substances that killed germs. Today medicines that are used to kill those germs known as bacteria are called antibiotics. The Makah people, who lived on the Olympic Peninsula of what is now Washington State, used yarrow as an antibiotic. The Yurok of California used rhizomes, or rootlike underground stems, of ferns as

▲▼▲▼▲▼▲▼▲▼▲▼▲▼▲▼▲▼▲▼▲▼▲▼▲▼▲▼▲▼▲▼▲▼▲▼▲▼

SPIDERWEBS

American Indians of some tribes packed wounds with spiderwebs to stop bleeding and to prevent them from becoming infected. Modern scientists have discovered that as spiders spin silk for their webs, they excrete an antiseptic (germ-killing) coating on the strands of silk. Some researchers are now testing the webs of different types of spiders to learn more about the chemicals that coat the silk and what bacteria they are most effective against.

Spiderwebs have antiseptic, or germ-killing, properties. Some American Indians put them on cuts and other wounds. *(William Radke/U.S. Fish and Wildlife Service)*

▼▲

an antibiotic. The Zuni of the Southwest used sage to treat foot infections. American Indians living in the Northeast relied on cranberries and blueberries for infection cures. Both contain arbutin, a phytochemical that modern medical researchers have found to kill germs.

The Aztec used sap from the maguey plant on open wounds. Substances in maguey increase the movement of water through the bacteria cell membranes. This movement is called cell osmosis. When maguey sap pulls water from bacteria cells, they die. The Aztec added salt to the maguey sap to make it work even better.

Mesoamerican physicians also used honey and salt to treat wounds. Modern researchers have found that honey is an antiseptic. It kills the bacteria that cause dysentery as well as staphylococci and

FATAL DISEASES

The first conquistadores, explorers, and colonists carried many new and deadly diseases with them to the Western Hemisphere. Some of these diseases were:

Bubonic plague is caused by bacteria. People catch bubonic plague by being bitten by a flea carried by a rodent, usually a rat. The first symptoms are swollen lymph glands. The bacteria spread throughout the body causing high fever, coughing, chills, and often death.

Diphtheria is caused by bacteria. When people have diphtheria, their throats become coated with a false membrane that prevents them from breathing. They suffocate to death.

Influenza is caused by a virus that infects the respiratory tract. Influenza causes coughing, a runny nose, sore throat, headaches, fever, and body aches. Flu

This engraving is based on a drawing that was made between 1562 and 1565 in what is now Florida. The first European disease epidemics there were introduced from the Caribbean islands. By 1607 smallpox had claimed the lives of half of the Timucuan people who lived in the area. *(Library of Congress, Prints and Photographs Division [LC-USZ62-045093])*

E. coli bacteria. Honey also contains substances that prevent fungi from growing. It dries microorganisms like maguey sap does. In addition, honey stimulates the white blood cells within the body to

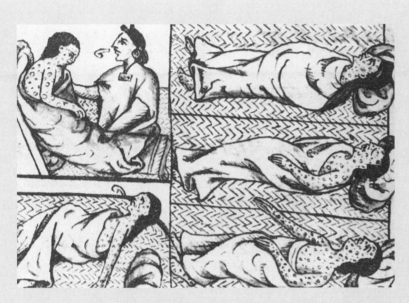

This drawing of a picture that was originally published in *Historia de las cosas de Nueva España* by Bernardo de Sahagún, shows Aztec people sick with smallpox, a disease carried to Mesoamerica by Europeans. By the time this book was written between 1575 and 1580, about half of the Indian people of Mesoamerica had died from European diseases. *(Rare Books Division, Library of Congress)*

can be a deadly disease, especially for the very old and the very young.

Malaria is a disease that is caused by tiny parasites. It is transmitted by the bite of a mosquito. Its symptoms are extreme chills and fever. It also causes the skin to turn a yellow color. It can be deadly.

Measles is a serious viral infection of the respiratory tract that causes coughing, sore throat, fever, and an itchy rash.

Scarlet fever is a severe illness. It is caused by a bacteria and causes a skin rash, sore throat, high fever, and vomiting.

Smallpox causes fever, headaches, and severe weakness. It also causes skin eruptions (pox) that eventually scab over. When the scabs fall off, scars remain. It was the most deadly disease carried to the Americas from Europe.

Typhus is a serious disease that causes a high fever that lasts a long time. It also causes sores and swelling of the intestines.

Typhoid fever is caught by eating food or drinking water that contains *Salmonella typhi* bacteria. It causes a high fever that lasts a long time. It also causes sores and swelling of the intestines.

destroy germs. Honey also contains small amounts of hydrogen peroxide, a wound cleaner that is used today.

EUROPEANS AND DISEASE INVADE THE AMERICAS

The first major epidemic of European diseases in the Americas started with Christopher Columbus's second voyage to Hispaniola in 1493. In the hold of his ship were farm animals that were infected with the influenza virus. (Influenza is commonly called flu today.) By 1520 the Spaniards had unleashed huge epidemics of many diseases throughout the Americas.

At first the germs were passed from Europeans to Indians. Soon they were passed from Indian to Indian. Entire villages of American Indian people died from European diseases, and some tribes were nearly wiped out. Many American Indian people died from European diseases without ever seeing a European.

IMMUNITY AND DISEASE

Because American Indians had never encountered European diseases before, they had no cures for them. They could not avoid catching these diseases because their bodies had not developed immunity to them. The body's immune system protects the body against viruses, bacteria, and fungi. It is composed of the bone marrow, the thymus gland, the lymph system, the spleen, and the tonsils. These all work together to recognize large proteins on the surface of disease-causing germs. These large proteins are called antigens. Each disease has a different antigen signature.

The immune system signals the white blood cells to begin making antibodies. Antibodies attack antigens and kill germs. It takes time for the immune system to recognize a new type of disease germ and come up with an antibody that will destroy it. People who have no immunity to a disease may die before their immune systems can make enough antibodies to help them fight it.

Once a person has survived a disease, some of the antibodies for that disease remain in the body. The next time the person is exposed to the same type of germs, the

Eight out of 10 Tsimshian Indians living on the Skeena River in British Columbia caught smallpox between 1860 and 1863. No matter how skilled American Indian healers were, they could do nothing to stop the epidemics. This picture of a Skeena River medicine man was taken between 1900 and 1930.
(Library of Congress, Prints and Photographs Division, Frank and Frances Carpenter Collection [LOT 11453-3, no.13 [P&P])

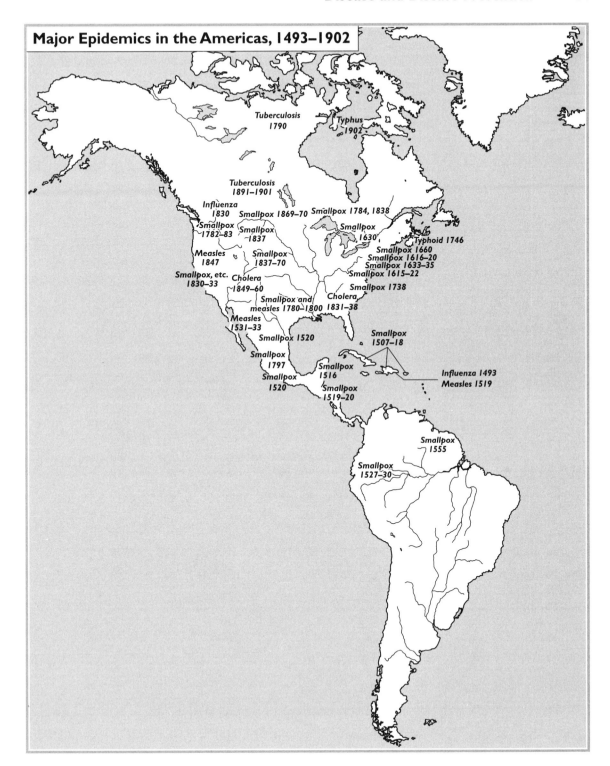

Major Epidemics in the Americas, 1493–1902

Tuberculosis
1790

Typhus
1902

Tuberculosis
1891–1901

Influenza
1830

Smallpox 1869–70   Smallpox 1784, 1838

Smallpox
1782–83

Smallpox
1837

Smallpox
1630

Typhoid 1746

Measles
1847

Smallpox
1837–70

Smallpox 1660
Smallpox 1616–20
Smallpox 1633–35
Smallpox 1615–22

Smallpox, etc.
1830–33

Cholera
1849–60

Smallpox 1738

Smallpox and
measles 1780–1800

Cholera
1831–38

Measles
1531–33

Smallpox 1520

Smallpox
1507–18

Smallpox
1797

Smallpox
1516

Smallpox
1520

Smallpox
1519–20

Influenza 1493
Measles 1519

Smallpox
1555

Smallpox
1527–30

antibodies quickly signal the immune system to make more antibodies just like them. The germs are destroyed and the person remains healthy.

Europeans had been exposed to the germs that caused smallpox and other diseases. A number of them had acquired immunity to

TIME LINE	
1493	On his second voyage Christopher Columbus lands on the island of Hispaniola, bringing livestock in order to start a colony there. Influenza germs from the animals cause an epidemic. It sweeps through the island, killing many Indians.
1507–1518	Two waves of smallpox kill from one-third to one-half of the American Indians in what are now Cuba, Haiti, and Puerto Rico. In 1516 Indian traders carry the disease to the Yucatán Peninsula of what is now Mexico, where it kills many Maya.
1519	The Spaniards bring germs that start a smallpox and measles epidemic to Santo Domingo in the Caribbean. One-third to one-half of the American Indian people there die. The epidemic spreads to what are now Puerto Rico, the Antilles Islands, and Mexico. In Puerto Rico alone 180,000 Indian people die.
1519–1520	Smallpox reaches what is now Guatemala. An American Indian who survived recorded: "Great was the stench of the dead. After our fathers and grandfathers succumbed, half of the people fled the fields. The dogs and the vultures devoured the bodies."
1520	Smallpox germs enter what is now Mexico at the port of Veracruz on the ship of Pánfilo de Narváez. The disease quickly spreads to Tenochtitlán, the Aztec capital. Within 10 years, 33 percent of the Mesoamerican Indian people die from European diseases. Within 75 years, 95 percent of them die from the European diseases.
1521	Smallpox spreads south through Mesoamerica and South America.

these diseases. In Europe many of these diseases had become childhood diseases. When the children became adults, they were immune to these childhood diseases. Today children are given vaccinations to make them immune from these diseases.

1527–1530	Smallpox arrives in the Inca Empire. The Inca ruler Huayna Capac dies from it. As many as 200,000 Inca people are killed by the disease.
1540	The Spanish explorer Hernando de Soto travels through the Southeast. It is believed that diseases spread by his party and the animals that they brought with them for food eventually killed about 75 percent of the American Indians in the Southeast.
1560	Another wave of smallpox kills so many Native people in Brazil that the Portuguese can no longer rely on Indian slaves to cut sugarcane on the plantations they have established. They import slaves from Africa.
1585	English settlers on what is now Roanoke Island in Virginia spread diseases, and many Indian people living nearby die. Some historians believe the settlers carried malaria germs.
1617–1619	A disease that is thought to be smallpox sweeps through what is now the Massachusetts Bay. Nine out of 10 Indian people die. The disease is believed to have been brought by the crew of a European fishing or slaving boat.
1620	The Pilgrims arrive on the *Mayflower* and start Plymouth Colony. They are helped by Tisquantum (Squanto), a Wampanoag Indian, whose entire village died from a European disease. The Pilgrims, who bring more European disease germs to the Americas, believe the epidemics are an act of God. They take them as a sign that they, not the Indian people, are meant to live on the land.

4

Plant Medicines of North America

Indian healers throughout the Americas gathered plants that they used to cure sickness. They also planted and harvested many types of plants for medicine. They had many ways to make medicines from these plants. Most often they began by drying and grinding the roots or leaves that contained the medicinal chemicals. Then they boiled these powders in water or allowed them to sit in warm water. This released the healing substances. Less often they used fresh plants or whole plants. To reduce swelling and pain, they crushed plants to make a poultice that they put on the external injury. Sometimes they dried plants and burned them so that patients could inhale the smoke.

American Indian doctors used a number of ways to administer, or give, medicine to patients. Some healers injected medicines beneath the skin with syringes. North American Indians made a syringe from a small animal bladder and a thin, hollow bird bone. They sharpened and beveled, or angled, one end of the bird bone. Then they attached the bladder filled with medicine to the opposite end of the bone. The healer squeezed the bladder and injected medicine beneath a patient's skin. Sometimes American Indians used larger syringes to give patients enemas. Mesoamerican Indians made syringes with rubber bulbs.

Some North American Indian healers used a suppository to give patients medicine. A suppository is a small plug of medicine that is inserted into the body, usually into the anus. Indians of the Northeast made pills. They ground moist cranberry bark and shaped it into small pellets. They took these pills to relieve muscle spasms, or

American Indian healers were skilled in making medicines from plants. The wigwam style of house indicates that the medicine man was from a Northeast culture. The metal pots at his side were popular trade items used by fur traders. This picture was made by Seth Eastman in the 1850s. Seth Eastman was the grandfather of Charles Eastman, the first American Indian physician to be trained in a non-Indian medical school. *(Courtesy of the National Library of Medicine)*

cramps. Sometimes American Indians used gum as medicine for problems such as headaches and toothaches. North America Indians chewed pine needles to relieve sore throats and coughing. Besides soothing the symptoms, the needles provided vitamin C.

SOME NORTH AMERICAN INDIAN MEDICINES

The Indians of North America used as many as 2,564 different types of plants to treat illness. In order to develop plant-based drugs that worked, they needed to understand the different effects that plants had on humans. They also needed to know how much of a plant substance to use in order to treat illnesses. Giving a patient too little medicine would not cure the sickness. Giving the person too much of a plant medicine might result in death. Chemicals contained in many medicinal plants are poisonous when people eat too much of them.

Cascara Sagrada

This shrub, which is also called buckthorn, works as a laxative. It contains chemicals called glycosides that make the intestine contract. The Kootenai of the Plateau region and California tribes made it into a tea.

Spanish missionaries gave the plant its name, which means "sacred bark." Perhaps they picked this name because the plant was much milder than European laxatives. Today cascara sagrada is one of the most common ingredients in over-the-counter laxatives.

Coneflower

For centuries the Indians of the Northern and Southern Plains used a plant called coneflower, or *Echinacea*, to treat infections caused by viruses. Indians of the Great Plains tribes relied on *Echinacea* to treat blood poisoning. Two chemical compounds in the root of the coneflower plant fight viruses by boosting the effectiveness of interferon. Interferon is an antiviral compound that the body makes to fight infections. Yet another phytochemical in coneflower makes it difficult for viruses to reproduce. Today echinacea has become a popular herbal cold and flu remedy.

Coneflower was used by the tribes of the Great Plains as an antiviral medicine. *(Gary M. Stoltz/U.S. Fish and Wildlife Service)*

Foxglove

North American Indians used the American foxglove plant to treat heart disease. The phytochemicals in American foxglove that act upon the heart are called glycosides. They increase the strength of the heart's contraction. The stronger the heart muscle contracts, the more blood the heart can pump. This improves the circulation of blood throughout the body. The glycosides in foxglove also slow the pulse rate, regulate the heart's rhythm, and rid the body of excess fluid.

American foxglove was a very strong medicine. American Indian healers were able to give their patients the correct dosage of foxglove so that it helped their hearts but did not make them sick or cause them to die. Digitalis, a popular medication prescribed by modern doctors for congestive heart failure, is made from the foxglove plant.

Lady's Slipper

Lady's slipper is the name given to many species of plants that belong to the orchid family. These plants grow from Canada to the southern part of what is now the United States. American Indians found that the roots and rhizomes of some kinds of lady's slipper contained substances that worked as a pain reliever. Rhizomes are rootlike, horizontal stems that grow beneath the ground.

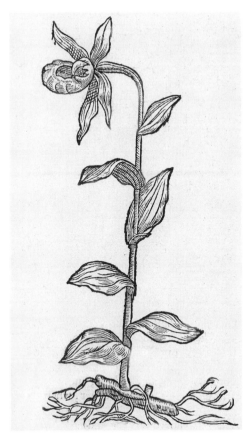

The lady's slipper plant shown in this drawing from an old herbal was used by American Indians of the Northeast to relieve pain. *(Library of Congress, Prints and Photographs Division [LC-USZ62-060477])*

The chemicals also worked as a sedative, or calming medicine, and as an antispasmodic, a medicine that stops seizures. A seizure is a condition that causes muscles to contract uncontrollably. American Indians harvested and dried the plants before mixing them with water to make a tea. Colonial physicians, who learned about lady's slipper from Indian healers, used it as a cure for sleep difficulties.

Mint

Plants that belong to the mint family contain oil in their stems and leaves that gives them a special smell and taste. The Cheyenne of the Northern Plains used mint tea to ease chest pains caused by

The Public Health Service (PHS) and Indian Health Service provide medical care to American Indian people in the United States today. The doctors who work for these agencies work together with traditional healers. In this picture a Navajo medicine man shows plant medicine to a PHS doctor in Gallup, New Mexico.
(Courtesy of the National Library of Medicine)

coughing. The Shoshone of the Great Basin region, the Navajo (Dineh) of the Southwest, and the Cree of the Subarctic used mint tea to treat cold symptoms. The Paiute of the Great Basin and the Kiowa of the Plains chewed the leaves to soothe sore throats. Mint in the form of menthol is a common ingredient in today's cough drops.

The Menominee people of the Northeast applied a mint poultice to the chest to treat pneumonia, much like the menthol chest rubs used today. People of Great Basin tribes applied poultices of mint leaves to aching and swollen joints as a rheumatism or arthritis treatment. Other tribes did this as well. Today many creams and rubs for aching muscles and joints contain oil from mint plants.

Indians throughout the Americas used mint for stomachaches. They included the Dakota of the Great Plains, the Mohegan and Chippewa (Anishinabe) of the Northeast, and the Washo of the Great Basin. Sometimes they chewed on mint leaves, but most often they brewed the mint leaves into a tea.

Sassafras

American Indians used the root covering and bark from the sassafras tree trunk for medicine and to flavor food. Sassafras is a tree that grows in the Northeast and Southeast. Its leaves, bark, and roots contain oil that has a distinct smell.

The Cherokee of the Southeast used sassafras as an intestinal worm medicine and for colds. The Lenni Lenape (Delaware) and the Mohegan of the Northeast drank sassafras tea as a tonic to keep them healthy. The Seminole of the Southeast used it to cure diarrhea and vomiting as well as for a mouthwash and gargle. The Aztec of Mesoamerica also used sassafras as a medicine.

During the Civil War, which began in 1861, army doctors used sassafras to treat soldiers with measles, pneumonia, bronchitis, or colds. Germans who lived in Pennsylvania drank sassafras tea to reduce fevers.

Sweet Flag

Sweet flag plants grow in wet soil at the edges of ponds, lakes, and streams. American Indians dug the rhizomes from sweet flag plants and used them as medicine. People of the Great Plains chewed sweet flag rhizomes to treat coughs and colds. Indians of the Northeast drank sweet flag tea as a cold medicine and gargled with the tea to cure sore throats.

Some American Indians used sweet flag for toothaches. The sweet flag rhizome contains phytochemicals called alkaloids that give it a bitter taste. These alkaloids also give the plant its medicinal qualities.

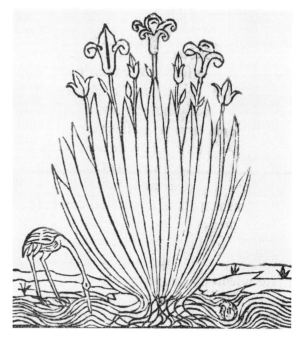

Sweet flag grows in Europe and in North America. It was used as medicine in both places. American Indians used sweet flag for sore throats, coughs, and toothaches. (Library of Congress, Prints and Photographs Division [LC-USZ62-339])

Willow

American Indians of the Northeast used the American black willow, or pussy willow, to make a tea they used to reduce fever, treat pain, and decrease swelling. The bark of American black willow contains salicin, a chemical that the body breaks down to form salicylic acid. Other pain medicines with salicin that American Indians used were white poplar and birch. Salicylic acid is the main ingredient in aspirin.

Wintergreen

American Indians of the Northeast and Southeast made tea from the leaves of wintergreen, a low-growing shrub. They used this tea to treat colds. The Iroquois and Lenni Lenape of the Northeast made poultices of wintergreen leaves to treat joint pains. Methyl salicylate, an oil in the wintergreen plant, has been found to be an antiseptic and an analgesic, or pain reliever. Today wintergreen is used as a food flavoring and is an ingredient in analgesic rubs used to treat sore muscles and joints. Eating large amounts of wintergreen can lead to poisoning.

Witch Hazel

Witch hazel is a tall bush that grows in eastern North America. American Indians used it for an astringent. An astringent draws together (contracts) the soft tissues of the body. Indians of the Northeast rubbed a solution of witch hazel and water on the skin to treat poison ivy and skin irritations. They also used it to treat minor burns, insect bites, stings, and bruises. European colonists adopted witch hazel as a medicine and sold it at pharmacies. Today witch hazel remains a common home remedy.

INDIAN MEDICINE BECOMES COLONIAL MEDICINE

Colonists in North America quickly came to rely on the plant medicines that American Indians had used for centuries. During the Revolutionary War, which began in 1775, army doctors carried standard medicine kits. American Indians had invented many of the medicines that the doctors used to treat soldiers. Continental physicians used the highly poisonous white hellebore, or Indian poke, as a laxative and narcotic. (For the most part American Indians had used hellebore as a poultice to relieve the pain of sore muscles.)

Army physicians carried boneset, or Indian sage, which American Indians used to reduce fevers, as a laxative, and as a treatment for muscle spasms. (Indian sage contains a volatile oil and a glycoside, which provide its medicinal qualities.) Continental soldiers were also treated with jalap, or bindweed, which American Indians used as a laxative, and datura, a plant that was used to reduce feelings of pain.

▲▼▲▼▲▼▲▼▲▼▲▼▲▼▲▼▲▼▲▼▲▼▲▼▲▼▲▼▲▼▲▼▲▼▲▼

LEWIS AND CLARK'S AMERICAN INDIAN MEDICINES

In 1804 when Meriwether Lewis and William Clark set out across North America to discover a northwest passage, they carried a medicine kit. They purchased 31 different medicines in Philadelphia. Many of the drugs that they bought were American Indian medicines. These included cinchona, a bark from Peru that was used to treat fevers; ipecac, a substance that induced vomiting; and laxative pills that were called "thunderbolts" and contained jalap.

▼▲▼▲▼▲▼▲▼▲▼▲▼▲▼▲▼▲▼▲▼▲▼▲▼▲▼▲▼▲▼▲▼▲▼▲▼

Later, more than 200 plants that American Indians used to treat diseases became part of the *U.S. Pharmacopoeia,* an official book that lists all effective medicines and their proper doses. The first official *U.S. Pharmacopoeia* was written and authorized by the professional medical community in 1837. Most non-Indian physicians used many American Indian plant remedies to treat their patients until the early 1900s.

In the early 1800s non-Indian botanical, or herb, doctors, began using American Indian plant medicines to treat patients. Many of their patients were afraid of the medicine practiced by formally trained American physicians. These educated physicians relied on removing large amounts of blood from patients and giving them harsh laxatives. They also burned patients' skin until it blistered and became infected. A number of patients died from the treatments they received instead of their diseases.

Colonists who lived in the Northeast trusted in Indian remedies so much that they began buying bottles of what they thought were American Indian medicines. Instead they were fooled into buying useless remedies made by non-Indians. They included Dr. Kilmer's Indian Cough Cure and Consumption Oil; Kickapoo Indian Cough Cure, Indian Oil, and Sagwa; Wigwam Tonic; Comanche War Paint Ointment; and Seminole Cough Balsam. About 60 percent of the hundreds of tonics that people could buy without a prescription had pictures of American Indians on their labels to make people think that American Indians made them. Some contained American Indian plant medicines, but most were made from alcohol, sugar, and water.

Over-the-counter plant medicines were called patent medicines. They received this name because their manufacturers registered their medicine bottles and labels with the U.S. Patent Office. By 1859 yearly sales of patent medicine topped $3.5 million. Later the U.S. government levied a special tax on them to help fund the Union army in the Civil War.

In 1906 the U.S. Congress passed the Pure Food and Drug Act. This law strictly regulated patent medicines and put many patent medicine companies out of business. Pharmaceutical companies began using chemistry to make drugs and turned their attention away from plant medicines even though about half of the prescription medicines taken today are made from plants.

Recently medical researchers have begun taking a second look at North American plant medicines. Synthetic (manufactured)

In the 1800s non-Indian businesspeople patented the Indian designs and names on the medicines that they sold. A patent is a government document that gives the person to whom it is issued the sole right to make a product. Red Jacket, a Seneca chief born in about 1756, had no connection to Red Jacket Stomach Bitters. *(Library of Congress, Prints and Photographs Division [LC-USZ62-55635])*

▲▼

SOFT DRINKS

Soft drinks are carbonated drinks that do not contain alcohol. Sometimes they are called soda or pop. North American colonists made root beer from sassafras, wintergreen, and birch. They also used sarsaparilla drinks as tonics. American Indians had used these plants as medicines for centuries. Considered to be medicine, soft drinks were first sold in drugstores in the early 1830s. Root beer was one of the first soft drinks to be sold in this way.

Sarsaparilla became a popular ingredient of soft drinks in the 1800s. Decorating the border of this label for Bristol's Sarsaparilla are drawings of sarsaparilla plants. *(Library of Congress, Prints and Photographs Division [LC-USZ62-057814])*

▼▲▼

antibiotics have been used so much that a number of germs are becoming resistant to them. Some scientists believe that the phytochemicals in plant medicines may prove to be good alternatives.

Scientists at the U.S. National Cancer Institute also believe that American Indian plant medicines may hold the key to finding a cure for cancer. For hundreds of years American Indians of the Northwest made a tonic from the needles of the Pacific yew tree. In 1960 the National Cancer Institute found that chemicals in this tree worked as an anticancer drug that stopped the growth of tumors. Today this drug, which is called paclitaxel and is sold under the brand name

Taxol, is credited with saving many lives. The U.S. government has established the National Center for Complementary and Alternative Medicine as part of the National Institutes of Health. This agency serves as a leader in researching plant medicine cures.

According to U.S. law, herbs that are sold without a prescription must be called dietary supplements. People in the United States buy $10 billion worth of dietary supplements each year. Many Americans buy and use over-the-counter herbs as medicine. In 2001 U.S. consumers spent $39,700,408 on the American Indian remedy coneflower and $10,279,853 on cranberry pills.

5

Plant Medicines of Mesoamerica

The physician-scientists of Mesoamerica systematically studied plants in order to discover new remedies. Spaniards who cataloged the plant medicines of the Aztec after conquest listed about 1,200 plants that the Aztec used as medicines. The Aztec established an empire in what is now central Mexico in about A.D. 1100. The Maya, whose culture flourished starting in about 1500 B.C. in the lowlands of Mesoamerica, used many of the same plant medicines as the Aztec did. Modern researchers believe that the people of Mesoamerica made use of at least 1,500 different plant medicines.

SOME MESOAMERICAN INDIAN MEDICINES

Many of the Indian people of Mesoamerica grew medicinal plants for minor health problems in their own gardens. They also bought plant medicines in the marketplaces located in the center of major cities. Aztec patients whose illnesses were more severe received treatment at hospitals by doctors who specialized in herbal medicine.

Agave

The Aztec called this desert plant *metl*. It consists of a thick cluster of gray-green leaves that are 10 to 18 inches long. These thick, fleshy leaves store moisture for the plant to use during dry periods. Mesoamericans used agave sap as a laxative. They also rubbed it on their skin to treat chapped lips, burns, rashes, and sunburns. The Aztec used agave sap to treat wounds as well because agave has antiseptic, or germ-killing, properties. Scientists have found that two chemicals in agave, polysaccharides and saponins, give this plant its healing properties.

Achiote

This tropical shrub was called *achiotl* by the Aztec. They used achiote to treat fevers and diarrhea. They also used this plant as a diuretic, a medicine that removes excess fluid from the body in the form of urine. The Aztec flavored chocolate drinks with achiote and also used it to dye clothing. Indians in South America's Amazon Basin mixed the oily red dye in the seed husks with rubber sap to make latex body paint that repelled insects. The chemicals that make achiote work as medicine are tannins, bixin, and tomentosic acid.

Arroyo Willow

Named *quetzalhuexotl* by the Aztec, arroyo willow contains salicin. Salicin is the active ingredient in aspirin. Mesoamerican doctors

Indian healers of Mesoamerica used many varieties of cactus to treat illness. They used the juice of the tall, thin saguaro cactus to treat snake bites and wounds. They cut a slice of the stem, heated it, and tied it over the wound. *(Courtesy of the National Library of Medicine)*

ground the bark and boiled it in water to make a tea that they gave to patients to treat fevers, headaches, and muscle and joint pains.

Chenopod

The Aztec called chenopod *epazote*. (It is often called pigweed in North America today.) Mesoamerican cooks boiled chenopod and ate it as a leafy green vegetable. People who had hookworms, a type of intestinal parasites, drank a tea made from *epazote*. The tea worked as a laxative to expel the worms from their intestines.

Chili Peppers

The Maya and Aztec ate chili peppers as a way to treat coughs and colds. They also ate chili peppers to help digestion and as a laxative. Chili peppers work in the digestive system by increasing the production of gastric (stomach) juices.

Mesoamericans also massaged chilies on their skin as a topical pain reliever. They rubbed chili peppers on the teeth and gums to stop toothaches, too. Chili peppers contain a chemical called capsaicin. When this chemical contacts the skin, it is a powerful irritant that causes the release of a chemical in the brain that is called substance P. This chemical tells the brain something painful is occurring. Eventually, when substance P is used up, the brain no longer recognizes the feeling of pain from that area of the body. That is why people sometimes notice numbness in their lips and mouth after they come in contact with the hotter varieties of chilies.

Today chili peppers are used in over-the-counter analgesic balms that are intended to relieve muscle and joint pain. The U.S. Food and Drug Administration has also approved the use of capsaicin in creams used to reduce phantom limb pain experienced by amputees and postoperative pain for mastectomy patients. Modern medical research has shown capsaicin to be effective in reducing pain from cluster headaches, shingles, and arthritis. When used repeatedly, cream that contains capsaicin reduces inflammation, or swelling.

Chocolate

The Aztec called the cacao plant from which they made chocolate *cacahuaquauit*. Chocolate was an important medicine for the Aztec. They used the oil from cacao beans as a lotion to prevent chapped lips and hands. The Aztec used cacao beans that had been ground and processed into chocolate as a germ-killing antiseptic. They also used chocolate as a diuretic and drug to stimulate contractions of the uterus during childbirth. Chocolate was used as a treatment for rheumatism (a swelling of the joints), snakebite, and wounds. Aztec doctors used chocolate to treat diarrhea and to cure melancholia (depression).

Modern research has shown that chocolate contains phenyle-phylamine, a chemical that is nearly the same as the one the human brain produces when a person falls in love. Other phytochemicals in chocolate are tannins and theobromine. Theobromine stimulates the body in the same way as caffeine. It also causes the kidneys to produce urine and dilates the small blood vessels, lowering blood pressure. Chocolate contains high levels of antioxidant chemicals called phenolics. These chemicals slow the oxidation of LDL in the body. (LDL is the saturated fat that clogs arteries when it combines with oxygen in the body.)

Corn Silk

The Aztec made the tassels on ears of corn into tea. They used it as a diuretic. Corn silk tea was also a treatment for urinary tract problems, including kidney stones. The phytochemicals that act as medicine in corn silk include saponins, alantoin, and sterols.

Jalap (Bindweed)

This twining plant grows in warm areas of Mesoamerica and in North America as well. One variety grows near Xalapa (Jalapa), a town in Mexico that gave the medicine its name. American Indians of Mesoamerica and parts of North America used jalap as a powerful remedy for constipation. They steeped the root in water to make a tea that was taken orally.

The Spaniards were so impressed by jalap's effectiveness as a cathartic that they introduced the medicine to Europe from Mexico in 1565. Jalap quickly became a popular constipation and indigestion remedy both in Europe and in the North American colonies. It remained a standard drug for non-Indian doctors until the early 1900s. If jalap is misused, it can cause rapid heartbeat. Today the U.S. Food and Drug Administration has classified it a dangerous remedy.

Juan Badianus, an Aztec, was educated by Spanish priests. Later he wrote a book about Aztec medicine that Spaniards presented to King Philip II of Spain in 1552. This herbal is now known as the Badianus Manuscript. It contains drawings of the parts of plants that grow above the ground as well as their roots. *(Emmart, Martin de la, Emily Walcott Emmart [trans.] Henry E. Sigerist [Fwd.] Badianus manuscript [Codex Barberini, Latin 241] Vatican Library: An Aztec Herbal of 1552, pp, 153, Plate 69 © 1940 [Copyright holder]. Reprinted with permission of the Johns Hopkins University Press.)*

Jimsonweed (Datura)

The datura plant, which the Aztec called *tlapatl*, was made into a tea to treat fevers. This tea was also used for chest pain and arthritis pain. (North American Indians used jimsonweed as an anesthetic, or pain reliever, as well.) The phytochemicals in jimsonweed are scopolamine, hyoscyamine, and atropine.

Aztec doctors made a poultice of datura and put it on the inflamed joints of people who had arthritis. Atropine was absorbed through the skin and provided pain relief by relaxing the muscles. Today atropine is an ingredient of some pain medicines that are rubbed on the skin. It is poisonous in the wrong dosage.

Mexican Oregano

This plant grew in the mountains of Mesoamerica. The Spaniards called it *oregano de la Sierra*. It is a different plant from the oregano that is used in Italian cooking. Mesoamericans made Mexican oregano into a tea that they used to cure coughs and stomachaches. They also used it to relieve gas.

Papaya

Aztec doctors called the tropical papaya tree *chichiualoxchitl*. Papaya trees produce sweet fruit. The Maya planted papaya trees in orchards. In addition to eating papayas as a food, they used papaya trees as a source of medicine. Sometimes they used papaya leaves as a bandage for wounds.

The Maya and Aztec drank papaya juice as a medicine to help digestion. An enzyme in papaya juice that is called papain breaks down protein. It also breaks down insect venom. American Indians used papaya on insect bites to reduce the effects of venom. Today papaya extract is used in the treatment of stomach and colon cancer.

Prickly Pear Cactus

The Aztec called the prickly pear cactus *nopal*. It served as a pharmacy for the Aztec and the Indians who lived in the desert Southwest. They used the watery pulp from cactus pads as a skin ointment and to reduce the swelling and pain of insect bites. American Indians of Mesoamerica ate prickly pear cactus pads for a diuretic and as a tonic. Modern research on animals shows that phytochemicals in prickly pear cactus boost the immune system and can slow tumor

The Aztec used prickly pear cactus as a heating pad. They drank the juice to rid the body of intestinal parasites and as a diuretic that rid the body of excess fluids. This drawing is a copy of one in the Badianus Manuscript. *(Emmart, Martin de la, Emily Walcott Emmart [trans.] Henry E. Sigerist [Fwd.] Badianus manuscript [Codex Barberini, Latin 241] Vatican Library: An Aztec Herbal of 1552, pp, 174, Plate 90 © 1940 [Copyright holder]. Reprinted with permission of the Johns Hopkins University Press.)*

growth. Prickly pear cactus also works in the intestines to slow the release of too much sugar and fat into the bloodstream. Mexican researchers found that prickly pear cactus helped to lower the blood glucose (sugar) levels of adult onset diabetics.

American Indians of the Southwest used prickly pear cactus pads as a kind of heating pad. After breaking off a cactus pad and burning off the spines, they would warm it over a fire. When it was hot, they would split it in half and apply it to aching joints. They used the same treatment for earaches and hemorrhoids. Hemorrhoids are enlarged and swollen veins in the area of the anus.

Spearmint

Early Spanish priests called spearmint *yerba buena*, which means "good herb." Mesoamerican healers made it into a tea. They drank the tea to calm upset stomachs, relieve intestinal gas, and ease headaches. Women who were giving birth also drank spearmint tea.

Sunflowers

The Aztec called sunflowers *chimalacatl*. They used sunflower seed tea to lower the body temperature of people with fevers. (American Indians of the Great Plains and Northeast used sunflower seed tea and sunflower oil as a cough medicine.) The active phytochemicals in sunflowers are a diuretic. They also help to rid the lungs of mucus. Sunflower seed's active ingredients are saponins and quercimeritrin.

HOSPITALS, DOCTORS, AND NURSES OF THE AZTEC

The Aztec built the first hospitals in the Americas. Aztec hospitals were located in all of the large cities. They were funded by the government and provided all citizens with many types of medical care. Like most hospitals today, these provided a wide range of services. Aztec hospitals were staffed with doctors and nurses as well.

The practice of medicine was a profession that was often passed from parent to child in Aztec families. Both women and men could be doctors. Aztec doctors specialized in different types of treatments. One type of doctor, the *tlana-tepati-ticitl*, used medicines that were taken by mouth or applied to the skin to treat sickness. Another type of doctor, the *texoxotla-ticitl*, performed surgery. Pharmacists, or druggists, called *papaini-papamacani* were in charge of gathering and preparing medicines.

Aztec nursing was also very organized. One type of nurse worked in hospitals. These nurses gave patients medicine and other treatments that doctors prescribed. Midwife/nurses were responsible for working with pregnant women. They were called *tepalehuiani*, which meant "to help someone" in Nahuatl, the Aztec language. Another type of nurse/midwife had more advanced training. This nurse was called a *temixihuitiani*, which means "to give birth" or "to cause someone to give birth" in Nahuatl. When a *temixihuitiani* encountered complications with a pregnancy that were beyond her knowledge and training, she asked a doctor for help.

In the Aztec Empire healing was a specialized profession. Here doctors treat a man who has been bitten by a spider. *(Rare Books Reading Room, Library of Congress)*

▲▽▲▽▲▽▲▽▲▽▲▽▲▽▲▽▲▽▲▽▲▽▲▽▲▽▲▽▲

AZTEC PILLS

Aztec pharmacists made pills for their patients. They wrapped the medicine in flower petals so that it would be easier to swallow. This is an example of the first "capsule" used in medicine.

▽▲▽▲▽▲▽▲▽▲▽▲▽▲▽▲▽▲▽▲▽▲▽▲▽▲▽▲▽

BOTANICAL GARDENS

The Aztec collected medicinal plants into large botanical gardens. Some of these plants were native to the Aztec Empire. Gardeners brought other plants from areas hundreds of miles away. Because the valley where the Aztec capital city of Tenochtitlán was located was

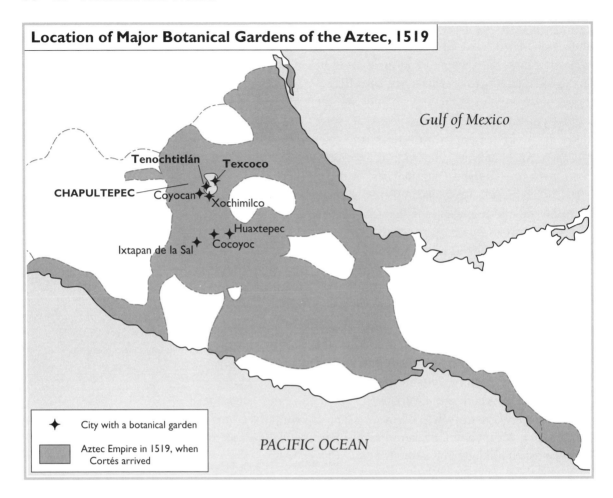

Location of Major Botanical Gardens of the Aztec, 1519

Gulf of Mexico

Tenochtitlán Texcoco

CHAPULTEPEC Coyocan Xochimilco

Huaxtepec

Ixtapan de la Sal Cocoyoc

✦ City with a botanical garden

Aztec Empire in 1519, when Cortés arrived

PACIFIC OCEAN

halfway between the tropical lowlands and the mountains, Aztec emperors were able to collect plants native to both of those regions. The Aztec routinely traded for medicinal plants with other Mesoamerican Indians, as did the Olmec and Maya before them. (Olmec culture arose in the lowlands of what is now Mexico in about 1700 B.C.) Trade gave the Aztec more plant varieties for their gardens. Trees and flowers grew in the gardens in addition to medicinal plants.

Montezuma, the Aztec emperor at the time of contact, had many gardens. Some of these were located in Tenochtitlán. Others were located several miles away, such as the gardens in Chapultepec. One of Montezuma's gardens was located near a hot spring north of Tenochtitlán. The emperor bathed here for his health. Another garden was planted at Huaxtepec, past the southern mountain range from

Tenochtitlán. There the Aztec grew tropical plants.

The Aztec lords who lived in cities throughout the empire also had gardens. Some of these were quite large. Nezahualcoyotl, the poet king of Texcoco between 1426 and 1474, built a garden that was located on a hill that overlooked the saltwater Lake Texcoco. His gardeners watered the plants with freshwater that was collected in a reservoir nine miles away. The walls of this reservoir were eight feet high. The water traveled to the garden in hardened clay pipes.

Many Aztec gardens were intended for the pleasure of the emperor and his nobles. They were also places for study and medical research. Aztec doctors were encouraged to give plants from the gardens to treat the illnesses of nobles. The patients reported on how the medicines had worked. The *papaini-papamacani*, or pharmacists, who were plant medicine experts, were supervised by the lord of the district in which they lived. In addition to giving patients medicines, they were expected to experiment with herbs and teach others how to use them.

AN INSPIRATION FOR EUROPEAN GARDENERS

The conquistador Cortés was impressed by one of Montezuma's gardens at Ixtapalapa, which was on the shore of Texcoco and located seven miles from Tenochtitlán. He wrote a letter to Spanish king and Holy Roman Emperor Charles V describing the magnificent garden. This letter was first published in Europe in 1522. Andrea Navagero, a Venetian statesman, planted the first private botanical garden the same year the Cortés letter was made public.

PLANT CLASSIFICATIONS

American Indians developed a formal system for classifying plants. They classified plants according to their form, their use, and their economic value. The form categories were trees, bushes, and herbs. The use categories included medicinal, food, and ornamental. The economic category divided plants according to whether they were used to make clothing, for building, or for other economic uses. The Aztec invented this system at least 400 years before Swedish botanist Carolus Linnaeus created the European binomial system for classifying and naming plants.

Aztec working people often had their own small herb gardens near their homes. They treated themselves and their families with plant remedies that had been passed down to them through their parents and grandparents. Those who could not grow their own plant medicines could buy them in markets. The conquistador Hernán Cortés wrote:

> There is a street of herb vendors, where you can find all of the medicinal roots and herbs offered by the soil. There are houses of apothecaries where they sell the medicines already made up in ointments and poultices.

Today many Mesoamerican people continue to use plant medicines. They buy them in stores called botanicas.

Francisco Hernández, who had been sent by the king of Spain to study Aztec medicine, visited several of the gardens, but focused on the one at Huaxtepec for most of the seven years he spent in Mexico. The Spanish priest Bernardino Alvarez founded a hospital on the grounds of this garden shortly after conquest.

Even though early conquistadores preferred to be treated by Aztec physicians rather than their own doctors, Spain sent more and more European doctors to Mesoamerica. Francisco Hernández, who was put in charge of these Spanish doctors in New Spain, began to belittle Aztec doctors and their plant medicines. He accused them of practicing a medicine inferior to that of Europe and tried to make certain that only Spanish doctors could treat patients.

No longer able to practice medicine officially, Aztec physicians continued to secretly treat their own people. Maya herbal healers did the same, as did other groups of Mesoamerican Indians. Many of the medicines that the American Indian people of Mesoamerica used hundreds of years ago continue to be used today. Modern researchers have found that many of the plant medicines that Mesoamerican healers used have medicinal benefit and are effective for treating disease.

6

Plant Medicines of South America and the Circum-Caribbean

American Indians who lived in South America and the Circum-Caribbean also discovered and used many plant remedies. The best-known of these medicines today are quinine, a malaria treatment that is made from the bark of the cinchona tree and coca, an anesthetic. South American and Circum-Caribbean Indian people used many other plant drugs as medicines. Some of these, such as yams and guaiacum, are used throughout the world today. Modern medicine uses many more ancient Indian plant medicines of the Amazon Basin. Scientists continue searching the tropical rain forest and talking to Native healers to learn about American Indian plant medicines that may someday be used to cure cancer, AIDS, and other life-threatening diseases.

Balsam of Peru and Balsam of Tolu

Balsam of Peru and balsam of Tolu come from related trees. (A balsam is a resin, or volatile oil, that oozes from cuts made in some plants. A volatile oil is one that rapidly changes from a liquid into a vapor.) The trees that produce balsam of Peru grow in the forests of what is now El Salvador as well as in other parts of Mesoamerica and northern South America. Balsam of Tolu comes from a similar tree that grows in the northern part of South America.

Indian people harvested balsam from the special trees by removing patches of bark from the trunk. They were careful to space these patches so that they did not kill the trees. Next they put pieces of

Balsam of Peru received its name because Spaniards shipped tons of this plant medicine from Lima, Peru, to Europe after conquest. European doctors once regarded balsam of Peru as a miracle cure.

cloth over the bare spots to absorb the sticky substance that oozed from the tree. When the cloths were soaked, they put them into a container of hot water. Because the resin is heavier than water, it would sink to the bottom of the container. Sometimes they made slits in the tree bark and collected the sap in cups or buckets.

American Indian healers used balsam of Peru and balsam of Tolu to treat skin diseases and sores as well as lung diseases. They also used it to kill parasites and to stimulate the heart and increase blood pressure. Balsam of Peru and Tolu contain phytochemicals that make it an antiseptic against bacteria. These balsams also kill fungi.

In 1820 both of these medicines became part of the *U.S. Pharmacopoeia,* an official list of medicines approved for use by doctors. Today balsam of Peru is an ingredient in suppositories that are used for hemorrhoids. Balsam of Peru is also used to make wound sprays, cough medicines, insect repellents, and as a fragrance in some cosmetics. Balsam of Tolu is an ingredient in some cough medicines.

Cat's Claw

Cat's claw is a vine that grows in the northern part of South America. Thorns on this plant look like cat's claws, and that is why the plant received its name. American Indian healers in what is now Peru used the stem covering and roots of cat's claw to treat painfully swollen joints. They also used it as an antiseptic medicine for wounds. Many South American Indians drank tea made from cat's claw as a tonic, a medicine taken to prevent disease.

Modern researchers have found that phytochemicals in cat's claw are alkaloids that kill viruses and reduce inflammation, or swelling. An alkaloid is a chemical that is made by a plant. All alkaloids contain nitrogen. They react with acids to make salts. The alkaloids in cat's claw also help the immune system to function better so that the body can resist disease. In the United States cat's claw is considered an herbal dietary supplement. Several U.S. drug companies have taken out patents for immune-boosting drugs based on cat's claw that may someday be used to treat AIDS and cancers, including leukemia and breast cancer.

Coca

Coca plants are small shrubs that grow in the mountains and forests of South America as well as in parts of Mesoamerica. American Indians began planting and harvesting coca plants at least 2,000 to 3,000 years ago. Farmers who grew coca traded the leaves with people who lived where the plant could not be grown.

The people of the Andes Mountains chewed coca leaves with lime (calcium carbonate). They made the lime by burning seashells or limestone. Lime released an alkaloid in the leaves that temporarily numbed whatever it touched. This alkaloid worked as a stimulant. A stimulant increases the action of the central nervous system, causing people to feel more alert and have more energy.

Leaves from the coca plant played an important part in the lives of the Inca. The Inca Empire was established in what are now Peru and parts of Bolivia in about A.D. 1000. Inca doctors used coca leaves as a numbing substance, or anesthetic. By rationing coca leaves to miners in mountain camps, the Inca government made sure they worked harder. The juice from coca leaves took away feelings of tiredness and cold and relieved hunger by numbing the stomach. The Inca also allowed nobles to use coca.

Spanish doctors first took coca leaves to Spain. By the late 1800s Europeans had learned to make cocaine from coca leaves. European doctors used it for an anesthetic when they performed surgery. Cocaine was the first local anesthetic used in Western medicine. A local anesthetic is one that only numbs a certain part of the body. People could buy cocaine drops at drugstores to treat toothaches. Modern doctors have used cocaine to treat eczema, a painful skin rash, and shingles, a herpes infection that causes painful outbreaks on the skin.

In the United States coca became the basis of a number of stimulating "nerve tonics," including Coca-Cola, which is named after the plant. An Atlanta druggist, John Pemberton, first made Coca-Cola in 1885. Pemberton called his drink "French Wine of Coca, an Ideal Tonic." Later he added African kola nuts

After the Spaniards colonized what is now Peru, they planted many fields with coca and sold the leaves. By 1550 many had made fortunes in the coca trade. In this 1904 etching, called "Invitation to Cocaine," the artist portrays the plant drug as a temptress, luring conquistadores into the drug trade and addiction. *(Courtesy of the National Library of Medicine)*

Cocaine was an ingredient of many popular "nerve tonics" sold in drugstores, starting in the mid-1800s. Coca-Cola was one of them. Fashionable people of the time believed that cocaine was a healthful stimulant. Today it is considered a health hazard and is an illegal drug. *(Library of Congress, Prints and Photographs Division [LC-USZ62-39705])*

to his recipe and changed the name. Cocaine was removed from the popular soft drink after the FDA banned the drug in 1903.

Today cocaine is considered an addictive drug and is included in the U.S. Drug Enforcement Administration's schedule of controlled substances. It can only be used by doctors for medical purposes. Modern doctors use manufactured versions of the numbing alkaloid in cocaine, such as procaine and novocaine, to treat medical conditions.

Curare

Curare is the name for the poisons that American Indians of the Amazon Basin make from vines that grow where they live. For centuries, they used these plants to make a substance to coat the tips of their arrows. Tubocurarine, a phytochemical in curare, causes death when it enters the bloodstream through a break in the skin. It works by blocking the electrical impulses traveling along the nerve cells that cause the muscles to move. When the muscles that control the lungs stop working, the victim stops breathing.

As long as curare does not enter the bloodstream it is harmless. Meat from animals hunted with curare-tipped arrows is safe to eat since the stomach does not absorb the chemicals in these poisons. Some Indians of the Amazon Basin used the same plants that they used as medicines to make curare. They rubbed them on their skin to treat infections and bruises. They also used the leaves of these plants to treat snakebite. American Indians of what are now Peru and Brazil used the roots of these plants to make teas to reduce fevers.

Modern surgeons give patients small doses by mouth of a drug made from curare plants to relax their muscles without causing them to lose consciousness, or awareness. This drug is called *tubocurarine chloride.* It is used in throat, stomach, and chest operations. Doctors also use curare to treat a disease called tetanus, or lockjaw, which is caused by bacteria. A toxin, or poison, that the bacteria makes causes the jaw and throat muscles to cramp so that people with tetanus cannot chew or swallow. Before curare was used to treat tetanus, many people died from the disease.

Guaiacum

Guaiacum is a hardwood tree that grows in the Circum-Caribbean. This tree contains a resin, or sticky substance, that American Indian healers used as a tonic. To make this tonic they pounded the tree's bark into a powder and put it in hot water. When a sick person swallowed this guaiacum tea, it made the person's throat feel warm and reduced swelling. It also relieved coughing.

After contact guaiacum quickly became a popular drug among non-Indian physicians. Today it is common ingredient in cough syrups. Guaiacol, a drug made from guaiacum, is used as a germ-killing antiseptic. It is also used as a local anesthetic. Guaifenesin, another drug that is made from guaiacum, is sold as Robitussin cough syrup. Today, guaiacum is also commonly used in a test to find unseen blood in stool samples.

Indian people in the Circum-Caribbean used guaiacum for sore throats and coughs. This picture of a twig from a guaiacum tree was originally published in Gerard's *Herbal* in 1561. *(Courtesy of the National Library of Medicine)*

Guarana

The seeds of the guarana shrub, which grows in the Amazon Basin, contain the phytochemicals caffeine and theobromine. (Theobromine is also found in chocolate.) Both of these substances are stimulants. The Guarani people of the Amazon Basin made medicine from guarana seeds by shaking them in sacks to remove their outer coverings. Next they ground the seeds into a paste, which they formed into sticks. They slowly dried these sticks over a fire for many days. When they wanted to make guarana tea, they grated the sticks into hot water. People of the Amazon used guarana tea to boost energy and to relieve pain. European doctors began using guarana as a headache remedy. Today guarana is used to make a popular soft drink in Brazil. It is sold as a dietary supplement in the United States.

Ipecac

Ipecac is a drug that is made from the roots of a shrub that grows in South America and parts of Mesoamerica. The name for this plant comes from an American Indian word that means "sick making plant." Native people of the Amazon Basin dried the roots of

The Spaniards believed that guaiacum was a miracle cure. They called it *lignum vitae*, or "wood of life." In this picture that was created in the late 1500s, Europeans are preparing guaiacum bark in order to make medicine for a patient. *(Courtesy of the National Library of Medicine)*

this shrub as well as its rhizomes (rootlike stems that grow underground). They powdered these and used them to make patients who had been poisoned vomit. Vomiting emptied their stomachs of poison. Indians of the Amazon Basin also used ipecac as medicine to treat intestinal parasites. The phytochemicals in ipecac are alkaloids.

For more than 300 years ipecac was one of the most used poison-control drugs throughout the world. Today many poison-control centers do not use or recommend ipecac because it can cause vomiting that lasts too long. In 2003 the U.S. Food and Drug Administration heard testimony from physicians who believed that ipecac should no longer be sold without a prescription because people who are poisoned should get professional medical treatment rather than using a home remedy.

Jaborandi

American Indians of the Amazon Basin used the leaves of the jaborandi tree as medicine to relieve chest congestion by coughing. They also used jaborandi to rid the body of excess fluid through urination and perspiration, or sweating. Because jaborandi flushed toxins from the system, many Indians of the Amazon Basin used it as an antidote to poisoning. The Tupi Indians of Brazil, whose name for the jaborandi tree means "slobber mouth plant," used it to treat dry mouth. The Guarani people of what is now Brazil used jaborandi to cure mouth sores.

In the late 1800s European doctors began using jaborandi to treat upper respiratory infections, such as flu and pneumonia. The active ingredient in jaborandi leaves is the phytochemical pilocarpine. In addition to triggering salivation and sweating, pilocarpine helps the nerves send messages to the muscles. Modern doctors use pilocarpine to treat glaucoma. Glaucoma is a condition in the eye that is caused by the buildup of too much aqueous humor, the jellylike substance that fills the center of the eye. When doctors put pilocarpine drops in the eye, they help contract the eye's pupil and relieve the pressure. Physicians also give patients pilocarpine pills to treat dry mouth.

Quinine

The drug quinine is made from the bark of a tree that grows in the mountains of Peru: the cinchona tree. The American Indian people of the Andes Mountains called the tree *quina,* or *quinquina.* They used it to treat fevers.

Today quinine is used to treat or prevent malaria. Malaria is a disease caused by parasites that are so small that they can only be seen with the help of a microscope. Mosquitoes that have these parasites carry them from person to person. The symptoms of malaria include chills, fever, and weakness. People with malaria also develop anemia, too few red blood cells. Some people who catch malaria die from this disease.

The active ingredient in quina bark is an alkaloid called cholorquine. It acts by slowing down the growth of malaria parasites in the sick person's red blood cells. Cholorquine is also given to people going to malaria-prone areas to prevent them from getting it. Modern doctors prescribe quinine for other types of fevers as

A worker in Ecuador ties baskets of cinchona plantings to be transplanted. After the Spaniards learned that cinchona could be used as medicine to treat malaria, they grew cinchona trees commercially. *(Library of Congress, Prints and Photographs Division [LC-USZ62-95845])*

A ROYAL CURE

Malaria did not exist in the Americas until Europeans introduced it. In Europe the disease had been known for centuries. European doctors and their medicines could do nothing to cure malaria.

In 1638 the countess of Chinchón, the wife of a Spanish colonial official who lived in Lima, Peru, fell ill with malaria. Her Spanish doctor used some American Indian healing practices. He recommended that she drink tea made from the bark of the quinquina tree. More than likely he hoped to lower the countess's fever with this plant medicine. The countess took the quinquina bark medicine and became the first European to be cured of malaria with quinine. Scientists renamed the quinquina tree after the countess, calling it cinchona. Eager to seek his fortune, her doctor returned to Spain in 1648. There he sold the South American bark for $75 an ounce.

well. It lowers the body temperature by making the small blood vessels larger, or dilating them. Quinine also reduces pain by acting on the central nervous system.

Yams

Yams are tropical vines with heart-shaped leaves. They grow underground tubers. A tuber is a swollen root. American Indians of the Amazon Basin ate yams as food. They also used certain kinds of yams to stun fish in order to make them easier to catch. They used these

AN UNDERGROUND PHARMACY

Modern researchers have found that the type of yams that American Indians of the Amazon Basin used as medicine are filled with phytochemicals called saponins. One kind of saponin, called sapogenin, acts as a pain reliever and a calming drug. Dioscoretine, another saponin, helps to keep blood sugar levels normal. Three other phytochemicals in yams, disogenin, dioscorin, and dioscon, help the body to make sex hormones as well as steroids. Steroids are hormonelike substances that reduce the swelling, redness, and pain of inflammation. Steroids also decrease the body's immune system response and are used to treat diseases caused by the body's immune system attacking the body itself.

varieties of yams for medicine as well. Indians of the Amazon Basin used yams to treat the pain-fully swollen joints of arthritis. The Aztec of Mesoamerica made tea from wild yams, which they called *chipahuacxithuitl*. They used it to treat childbirth pain and epilepsy, a condition that causes seizures, or uncontrolled muscle spasms.

Modern drug researchers studied how American Indians in the Amazon Basin stunned fish with yams in order to find a plant source from which they could make steroids. Several steps are required in order to make inexpensive artificial steroids from yams. Steroids made from yams are used today to make hormones and birth control pills. They are also used to treat asthma, arthritis, and rheumatism as well as a number of other illnesses.

7

Surgery and Wound Treatment

American Indians were very skilled at performing many types of surgeries long before Europeans arrived in the Western Hemisphere. Surgery uses instruments to operate on people usually to repair damage to the body or to treat disease. American Indian surgeons of North America, Mesoamerica, and South America knew how to control bleeding. They used anesthetics and asepsis. An anesthetic is a substance that causes a loss of feeling in part or all of the body so that the person who takes it does not feel pain. Asepsis is a sterile, or germ-free, environment.

AMERICAN INDIAN SURGERIES ON THE BODY

American Indian healers routinely removed growths on the skin and eyelids of their patients. The Moche people, whose civilization arose in what is now Peru in about 200 B.C., were doing these simple surgeries by at least A.D. 600. Many of the operations that American Indians performed were much more complicated. They removed fluid from the chest cavity, performed skin grafts, and even performed brain surgery.

Most of the healers in the Hupa tribe that lived in the northern part of California were women. In addition to healing with prayers and ceremonies, they gave patients medicines and treated their wounds. *(Library of Congress, Prints and Photographs Division, Edward S. Curtis Collection [LC-USZ62-101261])*

Amputations

Evidence from pottery made by the Moche shows that they were able to successfully amputate limbs. The Aztec amputated, or removed, limbs as well. They also made artificial limbs to replace the ones that they had removed. North American Indian healers also removed limbs that were injured or diseased. Indian healers usually amputated the limb at the joint.

Arthrocentesis

Arthrocentesis is an operation to remove fluid from the knee joint. Too much fluid in the knee makes it difficult to move the joint and causes pain. Modern doctors treat this problem by puncturing the area with a needle to drain the fluid. Hundreds of years ago, Aztec doctors used a thorn to puncture the knee. This allowed the excess fluid in the joint to drain.

Cataract Surgery

Aztec doctors were also experts at removing cataracts from the eyes. People are said to develop cataracts when the lens of their eye becomes clouded. The lenses of the eyes are made from protein and water. As a person ages, some of the proteins clump together in the lens. Over time, as more proteins form clumps, it becomes difficult for the person with cataracts to see. Left untreated, this condition can lead to partial or total blindness.

Aztec physicians used small, thin pieces of obsidian, a kind of rock, as scalpels. They carefully removed the clouded lenses from the eyes of people with cataracts. This surgery allowed the people to go about their daily tasks.

Skin Grafts and Plastic Surgery

Skin grafts use skin from one part of the body to replace skin that has been torn or removed from another part of the body. Mesoamerican Indians grafted scalp tissue. The scalp is the skin that covers the head. The Chippewa

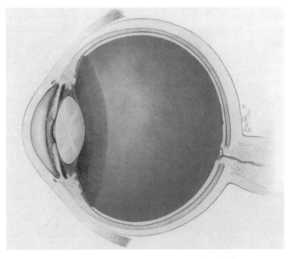

Cataract surgery requires great care and a delicate touch. The Aztec were experts in this type of surgery, which restores sight to people whose vision is clouded by cataracts on the lens of the eye. *(Courtesy of the National Eye Institute, National Institutes of Health)*

(Anishinabe) of northeastern North America performed surgery to repair torn ears. Aztec surgeons trimmed the ear tissue so that both sides of the tear matched up evenly and then they sewed them together.

Bernardo de Sahagún, a Spanish priest who lived in Mexico soon after conquest in 1520, wrote that Aztec surgeons treated wounds to the face so that no scars would form. If the patient's face did become scarred, the Aztec doctors would operate to correct the scars. When they operated they used hair from the head to sew the wounds together. The Aztec reattached patients' noses that had been injured. When this was impossible, they used an artificial nose.

Thoracentesis

Thoracentesis is surgery that involves puncturing the chest in order to drain infected fluid from the area between the lungs and tissue that surrounds them. This area is known as the pleural cavity. Sac (Sauk) and Fox (Mesquaki) healers of the Northeast punctured the pleural cavity with a long and slender thorn. They were careful not to make a hole in the lungs. Modern doctors use surgical instruments to perform the same operation and drain fluid from the chest.

AMERICAN INDIAN SURGERY ON THE BRAIN

American Indians of North America, Mesoamerica, and South America practiced a form of brain surgery that is called trephination. Ancient doctors removed part of the skull to relieve pressure or to repair an injury to a patient's head. Archaeologists, scientists who study the past, believe that thousands of ancient American Indian patients underwent this operation. More than half of the people who had brain surgery survived. Nine out of 10 patients who underwent this surgery in ancient Europe died from the operation.

The Paracas people, who lived in what is now Peru from about 1300 B.C. to A.D. 20, began doing trephination about 3,000 years ago. These first American brain surgeons used anesthetics to numb a patient's sense of feeling. They used scalpels made of copper, silver, gold, and combinations of these metals to cut the patient's scalp. When they had cut a flap of skin, they folded it out of the way. Then the American Indian brain surgeons sawed, scraped, or drilled through the skull. They controlled bleeding by holding hot rocks against blood vessels that had been cut.

Peruvian Trephination

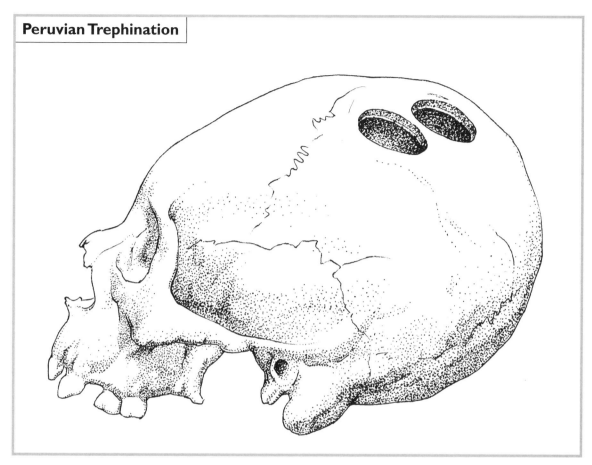

This skull shows evidenced of trephination, a type of brain surgery. It was found in Peru. The Indian people who lived there began performing brain surgery about 3,000 years ago. *(© Facts On File)*

After the surgery was finished, they covered the hole that they had made in the skull with a piece of dried gourd and thin sheets of gold foil. This would protect the brain while the bone grew back

▲▼▲▼▲▼▲▼▲▼▲▼▲▼▲▼▲▼▲▼▲▼▲▼▲▼▲

COTTON AND GAUZE

The Paracas physicians were the first people to use cotton gauze and loose cotton as a wound dressing. The cotton and gauze helped to keep the wound area free from germs and decreased the risk of infections.

▼▲▼▲▼▲▼▲▼▲▼▲▼▲▼▲▼▲▼▲▼▲▼▲▼▲▼

together. Finally they used needle and thread to sew the skin together to cover the wound.

South American doctors did more brain surgeries than other American Indians did. Inca doctors used trephination to treat headaches and to treat a condition that doctors today call depression. They used brain surgery to remove tumors, or growths, on the brain. They also used it to treat wounds to the head from battle. Sometimes they performed the surgery for religious reasons. (The Inca established an empire in the Andes Mountains in about A.D. 1000.) Archaeologists have found that some Inca patients underwent several trepanning operations. One person had survived five of them. In Cuzco, the capital of the Inca Empire, between 83 and 90 percent of the patients who had brain surgery survived.

The Olmec of Mesoamerica performed operations on the brain as well. Olmec culture flourished from about 1700 B.C. to about 400 B.C. Some scientists who study the past believe that the Olmec began experimenting with brain surgery before the Paracas people performed the operation. The Maya, whose culture arose in a nearby region of the Yucatán Peninsula in about 1500 B.C., are believed to have continued the process. Evidence of prehistoric brain surgery has also been found in parts of the United States and Canada.

SURGICAL INSTRUMENTS

American Indian surgeons performed most of their operations with scalpels. Scalpels are small, thin blades used for making incisions, or cuts, during surgery. Throughout the Americas Indian healers made

▲▽▲▽▲▽▲▽▲▽▲▽▲▽▲▽▲▽▲▽▲▽▲▽▲▽▲▽▲▽▲▽▲▽

SHARP INSTRUMENTS

Obsidian is a form of volcanic glass. It can be chipped, or flaked, to an edge that is the width of a molecule. Obsidian scalpels do not tear human cells as metal blades do. An incision made with an obsidian blade stops bleeding soon after it has been made. Healing begins shortly afterward. Only in the last half of the 20th century has Western medicine come up with laser technology that produces results similar to the obsidian scalpels that were used by ancient American Indian surgeons for thousands of years.

▽▲▽▲▽▲▽▲▽▲▽▲▽▲▽▲▽▲▽▲▽▲▽▲▽▲▽▲▽▲▽▲▽▲▽

scalpels from flint, chert, or obsidian. These stone instruments had a micro-sharp edge.

Some American Indian cultures made metal scalpels in addition to those made of stone. Paracas brain surgeons made scalpels from copper and other metals as well as from obsidian and flint. Later Moche metallurgists used silver to make scalpels. Moche culture arose in what is now Peru in about 200 B.C. These metal scalpels were

▲▼

SURGICAL STAPLES

Surgical staples help hold the skin together so that a cut will heal with little scarring. They serve as a replacement for sewing the wound or cut. American Indians of the Amazon Basin used the leaf-cutting ant to hold skin together during the healing process. When a patient had a cut on the skin, the Indian doctor would pinch the edges of the wound together so that they were closely matched. Next, the doctor held the leaf-cutting ant close to the wound, so that the ant would bite down on it.

Leaf-cutting ants were used because their large jaws could hold the edges of the cut together. Once the ants had bitten, the healer removed the ants' bodies, leaving the clamped jaws in place. When they were no longer needed, the healer removed these surgical staples. (Modern surgeons began using surgical staples in the 1960s.)

The people of the upper Amazon Basin used ants to hold the edges of wounds together. Modern scientists study the medicine of the Amazon tribes in order to find cures for many diseases. *(Library of Congress, Prints and Photographs Division, Frank and Frances Carpenter Collection [LC-USZ62-39418])*

▼▲

shaped like fans. The wide, flat end served as the blade. The Inca also made metal scalpels.

Inca and Aztec surgeons used forceps when they performed operations. Forceps are medical instruments that look like tongs. The Inca used forceps to remove tiny bone chips caused by head injuries.

HEMOSTATS

Hemostats are techniques and medicines that are used to stop bleeding. When Aztec surgeons finished cutting with stone tools during amputations and brain surgery, they sealed the blood vessels by holding heated rocks against them. The heat from the rocks caused the blood to clot and stop flowing. This way to stop bleeding is called cauterization. Although modern surgeons do not use hot rocks, they do cauterize blood vessels to control bleeding.

To stop bleeding, American Indians also used plant medicines on surgical incisions and on wounds. The phytochemical in these plants that stopped bleeding is tannin. Tannin activates the platelets in the blood. Platelets are responsible for clotting. The Kwakiutl of the North American Pacific Northwest used spiderwebs to stem the flow of blood in the treatment of wounds. The Plains Indians used puffballs, fungi filled with spores that resemble dust. They placed the spores into the wounds. This caused the blood to thicken.

ANESTHETICS

Anesthetics are substances that cause partial or total loss of sensation. Some anesthetics cause people to lose consciousness. American Indian healers used plant-based anesthetics to numb pain. They gave them to patients who had medical conditions that caused pain, such as broken bones and muscle soreness. They also used anesthetics when they performed surgery.

The Inca prepared coca leaves and applied them to the areas of the body where a patient was feeling pain. Inca physicians also had their patients eat coca before surgery.

Indians of southern Arizona and northern Mexico used peyote to dull the pain of large open wounds, snakebites, and fractures. They ground the root of the peyote plant, prepared it as a poultice, and applied it to the injured area. Peyote's anesthetic properties were so effective that in the 1800s U.S. Army surgeons used the plant as a painkiller as well.

NON-INDIAN ANESTHETICS

Before the mid-1800s, non-Indian doctors who performed surgery did not have effective anesthetics. Some doctors knocked patients out by hitting them in the jaw. Before 1847 and the discovery of ether, alcohol and opium were the most reliable ways non-Indian physicians had to numb their patients' pain. The high dosages of alcohol required to kill pain sometimes killed the patients. The same held true for opium.

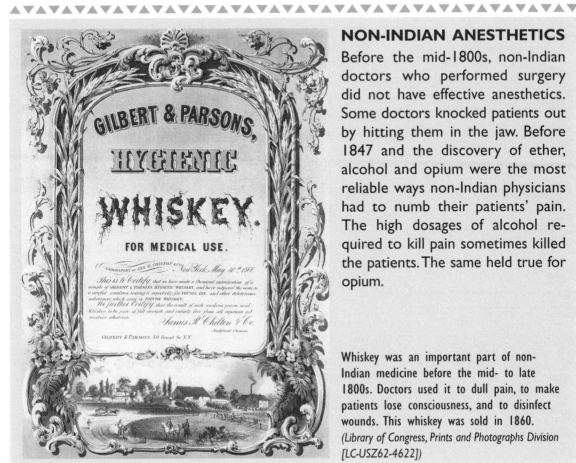

Whiskey was an important part of non-Indian medicine before the mid- to late 1800s. Doctors used it to dull pain, to make patients lose consciousness, and to disinfect wounds. This whiskey was sold in 1860. *(Library of Congress, Prints and Photographs Division [LC-USZ62-4622])*

American Indians living in what is now Virginia used Jamestownweed, or jimsonweed (datura) to relieve pain. Indian healers ground the root to form a plaster that they applied to wounds, bruises, and cuts. They had their patients drink tea made from the plants before setting their broken bones. After contact with American Indians, colonial doctors of North America adopted jimsonweed as an anesthetic.

STERILE SURGERY

When American Indians operated on patients or treated open wounds, they made certain that the incision was kept clean. They also used plant-based medicines to kill germs so that the incision or wound would not get infected. Antiseptics save lives by preventing infections, especially those caused by bacteria.

The Shoshone and Pauite, who lived in what is now Nevada, used cough root for a number of antiseptics, or disinfectants. Balsam fir served as an antiseptic for other North American tribes. One of the important South American antiseptics is the balsam of Peru. A substance in balsam of Peru killed bacteria that caused infections. American Indian healers routinely cleaned surgical incisions and wounds with water that had been boiled. Boiling water kills the germs that it may contain.

American Indians also used surgical drains to help prevent infections. Surgical drains helped wounds to heal faster too. A drain is an opening or a tube placed in a wound in order to provide a way out for dead cells that form pus. The Mescalero Apache of the Southwest treated deep wounds with drains. They made some from slippery elm and others from cotton that they had twisted to the size of a tongue depressor. The Apache placed a drain in the bottom of the wound and then sewed it in place. When the wound began to heal, they removed the drain.

Aztec physicians and those of other North American tribes removed foreign matter from wounds. This is called debridement. American Indian doctors applied clean bandages to the wound and changed them daily. Sometimes they packed the wound with eagle down (soft, fine feathers), the contents of a puffball or a spiderweb. Changing these dressings also removed the scabs from the wound and allowed it to heal faster. Indian healers also flushed wounds with medicine or water using a syringe.

Other Medical Treatments

8

American Indian doctors understood the parts of the human body and how they functioned. They used this knowledge to treat the diseases and injuries of their patients. North American Indians understood the skeletal system and were experts at setting broken bones. Mesoamerican physicians understood the workings of the heart and circulatory system long before Europeans possessed such knowledge.

The Aztec invented words to describe the different parts of the body so that doctors could talk with patients. These words also allowed them to discuss their patients' medical problems with one another. They had names for the organs, bones, and joints. They also organized the parts of the human body into systems. In contrast to the Aztec, Europeans at that time had little understanding of the internal organs and their functions.

In addition to treating patients with medicines that they made from plants, American Indian doctors used heat and massage to cure illnesses. American Indian healers helped women during pregnancy and birth. Native physicians of the Americas had a working knowledge of how to prevent the spread of disease that was much more advanced than that of Europeans at the time.

STEAM ROOMS

A steam room is an enclosed space where water is splashed onto a hot surface in order to make steam. Heat improves circulation and opens the pores in the skin so that toxins (poisons) are more easily flushed from the body by perspiration. Moist heat also helps to reduce congestion in the lungs.

In addition to using plant medicines, the Navajo (Dineh) used sweat baths and ceremonies to heal people who were sick. This photograph of a Navajo medicine man was made between 1872 and 1885. *(Library of Congress, Prints and Photographs Division [LC-USZ62-124567])*

Indians throughout North America understood the healing value of moist heat. American Indians who lived in the area of present-day Virginia used the sweat lodge for many disorders and health problems. These included sore muscles, arthritis, rheumatism, and chills. Great Plains Indians also used the sweat lodge. They built the fire to heat the rocks outside and brought the rocks into the lodge when they were sufficiently hot. Indians living in what is now Canada built similar sweat lodges. The Kwakiutl, a Northwest Coast tribe, used the sweat bath to treat illnesses. The Apache, Zuni, Navajo (Dineh), and other Southwest tribes used steam baths for similar reasons. Many American Indians continue the practice today.

American Indians, including the Thompson Tribe of the Northwest and the Choctaw of the Plains, steeped medicinal herbs in the water that they splashed on the rocks of their sweat lodges. They also placed medicinal plants on the hot rocks. Early non-Indian explorers called Choctaw sweat lodges "steam cabinets." One European writer suggested that colonists should adopt this practice and use it at least three times a year.

AN EFFECTIVE CURE

William Bratton, member of the Lewis and Clark expedition, had so much back pain, joint stiffness, and rheumatism that he could not walk. He was often the only member of the party who rode a horse. In May 1806 he was treated in a sweat lodge in Nez Perce country and was given mint tea to drink. Twice he was taken out of the lodge and plunged in cold water. Afterward he was able to walk with very little pain.

In addition to using steam rooms, American Indians of the Southwest heated prickly pear cactus pads and applied them to sore joints and muscles, much like a modern heating pad. Other tribes of American Indians sometimes soaked in hot springs to treat arthritis and other illnesses. Aztec nobility used hot springs north of the Aztec capital of Tenochtitlán as a healing spring.

Aztec and Maya steam rooms were small buildings that were made of stone. They were built next to people's homes. The Aztec called these steam rooms *temazcal*. Mesoamerican people built a fire against the outside wall of the steam room. When the rock wall was hot, they splashed water on the inside of the wall. The water evaporated, creating steam.

Often people tried a sweat bath to treat their illnesses before seeing a doctor. The Aztec used the steam room before prescribing medications or performing surgery on patients. The Aztec used steam baths to treat arthritis. Often they took plant medicines that helped to relieve pain before they went into the temazcal and right after they came out. Aztec women took a steam bath as they prepared to deliver a baby. The heat relaxed the muscles and ligaments of the pelvis so that giving birth was easier. Aztec women also went into a steam bath immediately after they had given birth.

MASSAGE

American Indians relied on massage to treat a number of illnesses. Massage manipulates the soft tissue of the body, including the skin and muscles. Modern researchers have found that massage decreases blood pressure, relieves muscle pain, and increases the circulation of the lymphatic system. This system carries waste products from the cells. Massage also reduces stress by causing relaxation. Reduced stress has been shown to help the body's immune system to fight illness.

Both the Maya and the Aztec of Mesoamerica used sweat baths to treat many common illnesses. The remains of this Maya sweat house show how Maya builders made them. *(Negative No. K5894; Courtesy of the Department of Library Services, American Museum of Natural History)*

The Maricopa and Akimel O'odham (Pima) people, who lived in what is now Arizona, used massage to relieve pain. Cherokee healers of the Southeast warmed their hands over hot coals before massaging their patients. They used massage to treat sprained muscles, pain, and menstrual cramps. The Pawnee of the Great Plains crushed the black rattle pod plant and mixed it with buffalo fat to produce a balm that they rubbed into the painful area.

The Aztec used massage in the steam bath. Bernardino de Sahagun, a Catholic priest, who described Aztec life during the early colonial period, wrote that Aztec doctors massaged a patient who had fallen. Aztec mothers were massaged in a steam bath soon after giving birth.

The Inca used massage to treat joint pain and lower back pain. They also used massage on patients before prescribing plant medicines or doing surgery on them. Inca doctors invented a special tool to use when they gave massages. It resembled a small baseball bat but was about 10 inches long. The Inca also developed special balms and oils for massages.

Another form of massage that American Indians invented is a widely accepted medical practice today. This is the Crede method of manipulation, a postpartum massage of the abdomen that helps women who have given birth to expel the placenta. It also helps the uterus to begin to contract.

BLOODLETTING

Bloodletting is the process of removing blood from a blood vessel. Today it is called *phlebotomy* and is used to obtain blood for testing. It is also used for donating blood. Indians of North America, Mesoamerica, and South America took blood from patients to treat headaches, heart pain (angina), swelling, and fevers. Unlike European physicians, who often bled a sick patient every day and sometimes removed as much as a fifth of the patient's blood at one time, American Indian healers removed only a small amount of blood. To do this they used a sharp stone knife, a porcupine quill, or a long thorn.

When a human being bleeds, the brain releases a hormone called vasopressin. This hormone lowers the body temperature, so that bleeding can reduce fevers. Aztec physicians knew that many headaches were caused by an excess of blood in the arteries in the brain or on the surface of the head long before European doctors

American Indians of some tribes used stone tools to remove small amounts of blood from patients, but they did not use bows and arrows for this purpose. European artists sometimes added details to their work from their imaginations. This drawing was made in 1699 in the Circum-Caribbean. *(Courtesy of the National Library of Medicine)*

understood this. Their belief that excess blood in the head was a cause of some headaches is supported by modern medicine. Aztec physicians advised their headache patients to rest and to avoid steam baths, as well as the sun, since heat is a vasodilator, dilating the blood vessels, and would only make the headache worse.

Among the Aztec drawing blood was a medical specialty. The Nahuatl, or Aztec, word for phlebotomist was *texoxotla-ticitl,* and the word for the knife used to make an incision was *itztli.* The Aztec phlebotomists knew the difference between arteries (vessels that carry blood away from the heart) and veins (vessels that carry it to the heart), and always drew blood from the veins. Aztec physicians were also familiar with taking the radial pulse. The radial pulse is the spot on the wrist at the base of the thumb, used to count the heart's beats.

BONE SETTING

American Indians knew how to set dislocated bones, bones that have torn loose from their joints. Healers of the Americas also set broken bones by moving the broken ends into place. (Left unset, broken bones heal crookedly.) Both the Maya and the Aztec knew how to massage a broken bone into place. Modern experts believe that the bone setting skills of American Indians before contact with Europeans were one of the most advanced parts of their medical knowledge.

North American Indians reduced, or put into place, dislocations of the foot or knee by tying one end of a leather strap to the foot and looping the other end around a tree limb. Lying on his or her back, the injured person pulled on the free end of the strap to apply traction to the joint until the bone popped back into place. Both North American and Mesoamerican Indians also did surgery to set bones when necessary.

▲▽▲▽▲▽▲▽▲▽▲▽▲▽▲▽▲▽▲▽▲▽▲▽▲▽▲▽▲▽▲

A MEDICAL SPECIALTY

Today traditional Maya bonesetters still practice this centuries-old medicine in parts of Mexico. Using their hands, they diagnose what bone or bones have been broken. As they work, they have the patient talk about what happened and work to soothe the person's fears. They use plant medicines to reduce swelling and pain. Then they use their hands to gently massage the bones into place.

▽▲▽▲▽▲▽▲▽▲▽▲▽▲▽▲▽▲▽▲▽▲▽▲▽▲▽▲▽▲▽

Once a bone had been set, it needed to be kept from moving until the break had grown together. American Indians used casts to keep the ends of a broken bone in place. The Shoshone and the Dakota, Lakota, and Nakota of the Great Plains used rawhide splints. Rawhide is animal skin, or hide, that has not been tanned. Indians

This Aztec doctor is bandaging an injured leg. The Aztec made casts to hold broken bones in place after they had set them. Several of the earliest Europeans in the Americas wrote that American Indians were more advanced in treating injuries and broken bones than European doctors were. *(Library of Congress, Rare Books Division)*

soaked the rawhide in water so that it was easy to bend. Then they placed the patient's broken leg on top of the wet rawhide and shaped a cast to fit the shape of the leg. When the hide dried, the healer attached it to the patient's leg with strips of leather.

Other tribes used splints as well. The Anishinabe of the Great Lakes wrapped broken limbs after they were set with heated birch bark. The birch bark served as a cast. When birch bark was not available the Anishinabe used the bark from the lodgepole pine. Other tribes used other kinds of tree bark for casts. Some tribes used wooden slats or sticks for casts.

If a patient had a broken back, American Indian doctors made a partial cast for the back

SURGICAL PINS

When broken bones fail to heal, modern doctors do surgery to implant a pin, or intramedullar nail, into the bone. Ancient Aztec surgeons used the same process hundreds of years before non-Indian surgeons. First they scraped the tissue from around the break or fracture and inserted a small piece of sap-filled wood or a piece of bone into the end of the broken bone to encourage new bone cells to grow. When they had finished, they covered the area with plants that prevented infections and stopped bleeding.

American Indian women who lived on the northern coast of South America near what is now the Orinoco River gave birth while leaning on a hammock that had been rolled so that it resembled a rope. Woman of other American Indian cultures gave birth kneeling, sitting, squatting, or standing. *(Courtesy of the National Library of Medicine)*

from bark. These back splints covered the body between the armpits and the hips and were wrapped with sinew or leather strips. The Indian doctor cut holes into the cast in order to be able to see how the patient's back was healing without removing the cast.

American Indians also made casts from wet clay and herbs. Small feathers, plant resins, rubber, and gum were also used to make casts. These casts dissolved by themselves by the time the bones had healed.

CHILDBIRTH PRACTICES

Obstetrics is the branch of medicine that deals with pregnancy and birth. American Indians made sure that women who were pregnant received proper care. When labor did not begin in a timely fashion, North American Indians used plant medications to start it. They also used plant medications to reduce pain during labor and to stop bleeding after child-birth.

Indian women throughout North America gave birth in a squatting or sitting position. This helped to open the pelvis and allowed gravity to help move the baby through the birth canal.

The Aztec sent a midwife to visit an expectant mother when she was six months pregnant. The midwife provided the woman with instructions about how to care for herself and the child she carried. Aztec midwives also gave expectant women a steam bath and massaged them. If the midwife learned that the fetus was in a breech position (the reverse position for a normal birth) she repositioned it with gentle massage. Before delivery the midwife would again take the expectant mother into the steam bath for washing and massaging. If the woman had a difficult labor, the midwife gave her medicine to strengthen her contractions. The medicine also helped to prevent too much bleeding after the

▲▼▲▼▲▼▲▼▲▼▲▼▲▼▲▼▲▼▲▼▲▼▲▼▲▼▲

CHILDBED FEVER

Unlike Europeans of the time, North American Indians were aware that women who had just given birth could easily catch infections from other people. Infection after childbirth, called childbed fever, or puerperal fever, killed many European women. American Indians of many tribes kept mothers and newborns apart from others and assigned one person to look after the mother and baby. Childbirth fever was rare among American Indian women.

▼▲▼▲▼▲▼▲▼▲▼▲▼▲▼▲▼▲▼▲▼▲▼▲▼▲▼

mother gave birth. For very difficult births, Mesoamerican surgeons performed cesarean sections, the surgical removal of a baby.

EMBALMING

When people died, American Indians of South America and Mesoamerica embalmed them. Embalming is the process of treating a dead body with preservatives in order to prevent decay. While embalming is not a medical treatment, it does require a great deal of knowledge about the human body.

Chinchoro embalmers of South America removed the internal organs from the body. Then they reinforced the spine, legs, and arms with wooden supports. After they had treated the organs to preserve them, they placed them inside the body. After this, they filled the body cavity with fiber and feathers. Finally they coated the body with clay. They sculpted and painted the clay to resemble the living person and placed a wig on the deceased person's head.

▲▼▲▼▲▼▲▼▲▼▲▼▲▼▲▼▲▼▲▼▲▼▲▼▲▼▲

THE FIRST AMERICAN MUMMIES

The Chinchoro people who lived in what is now Chile embalmed and wrapped their dead about 7,000 years ago in about 5000 B.C. Egyptians, who are well known for their practice of embalming and making mummies, began the practice during the First Dynasty in about 2000 B.C.

▼▲▼▲▼▲▼▲▼▲▼▲▼▲▼▲▼▲▼▲▼▲▼▲▼▲▼

▲▽▲▽▲▽▲▽▲▽▲▽▲▽▲▽▲▽▲▽▲▽▲▽▲▽▲▽▲

MAYA MUMMIES

The Maya mummified human remains, a practice that was closely tied to their religious beliefs. Maya culture flourished in Mesoamerica from about 1500 B.C. to about A.D. 1500. Although the Maya had no contact with the people of Egypt, their burial practices were remarkably similar. The mummies of Maya rulers were entombed in pyramids. Goods and servants were buried with them for their trip to the spirit world. The Maya pyramids also contained false chambers, similar to those of the Egyptian pyramids.

▽▲▽▲▽▲▽▲▽▲▽▲▽▲▽▲▽▲▽▲▽▲▽▲▽▲▽▲▽

The Inca of South America were embalming their dead by the 15th century. Inca embalmers removed the internal organs from the body. Then they washed the body inside and out and allowed it to dry. Next they packed it with cloth. After the body was embalmed, it was wrapped in more cloth.

Dentistry

Healthy teeth were important to ancient American Indians just as they are to people today. Decayed or missing teeth are painful. They also make it difficult for people to chew and digest food properly. As a result, the body may not get all the nutrients that it needs. American Indians with diets high in starches had more cavities in their teeth than those who obtained their food by hunting and gathering. This is because foods such as corn, beans, and squash contain more natural sugars than meat and wild plants do. Precontact Inuit people had cavities in about 1 percent of their teeth. In contrast, precontact Pueblo Indians, who ate a diet high in corn, had cavities in about 75 percent of their teeth.

American Indians took care of their teeth to keep them healthy. When a tooth did become decayed or infected, Indians of the Americas extracted, or removed, it. American Indians knew how to prevent and treat gum and mouth sores. They also knew how to prevent

▲▼▲▼▲▼▲▼▲▼▲▼▲▼▲▼▲▼▲▼▲▼▲▼▲▼▲▼▲▼▲

TOOTH DECAY

Starches (carbohydrates) break down into sugar in the mouth. Bacteria that live on sugar cause tooth decay. Bacteria are single-celled organisms. They make a sticky substance from sugar that coats the teeth. This substance is called plaque. When bacteria that live in the plaque break down food that has become stuck between teeth, they make an acid. This acid eats away the enamel of the teeth and forms cavities.

▼▲▼▲▼▲▼▲▼▲▼▲▼▲▼▲▼▲▼▲▼▲▼▲▼▲▼▲▼▲▼

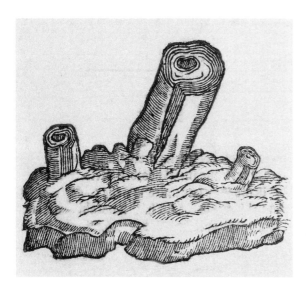

The Spaniards thought that a root that an Indian showed them growing in what is now Mexico was a miracle. They called it the Carlo Sancto root and wrote that it prevented tooth decay and cured toothaches. *(Library of Congress, Prints and Photographs Division [LC-USZ62-33999])*

and treat bad breath and how to whiten teeth. Ancient Mesoamerican dentists removed the parts of teeth that had cavities and filled them with pieces of jade or other semiprecious stones.

The Spanish conquistadores were impressed by Aztec dental practices. The Aztec established an empire in Mesoamerica in A.D. 1100. In 1571 King Philip II of Spain sent Francisco Hernandez, a physician, to Mexico in order to learn about Aztec medicine. He recorded that the Aztec used 49 plants to prevent tooth decay.

DENTAL CARE TO PREVENT CAVITIES

Indians throughout the Americas routinely brushed their teeth in order to remove plaque and bits of food that were stuck between their teeth. Many of them made toothbrushes by shredding the end of a twig and rubbing it on their teeth. Some Indians of North America used twigs from white pine trees. The Inca, who established an empire in what is now Peru in about A.D. 1000, made their toothbrushes out of the molli tree. The Aztec used a twig from the plant they called *tlatlauhcapatli,* in Nahuatl, their language. This plant had astringent properties. An astringent contracts, or draws together, soft tissues. In addition to cleaning the teeth, this Aztec toothbrush also tightened the gums and freshened the breath. The Aztec also cleaned their teeth by rubbing them with a soft cloth.

American Indians rubbed toothpastes and powders on their teeth in order to do a better job of cleaning them. In North America, the Mesquaki, a Northeast tribe, used white clay as toothpaste. The clay worked as a gentle abrasive that polished the teeth in addition to removing plaque. The Colville people of the Northwest used the ashes of alder trees in the same way.

The Aztec sometimes cleaned their teeth with a mixture of charcoal and salt. Both are mild abrasives. They used a toothpaste that they made from honey and white ashes, as well. They applied it to their teeth with a piece of cotton cloth. Then they used the cloth to rub away the plaque.

The people of northern South America, including the Inca, used the powdered bark of the balsam of Peru as a tooth powder. The Inca also used the root of a plant that resembled the dandelion to clean their teeth.

In addition to rubbing toothpastes and powders on their teeth, American Indians chewed different types of gums to clean their teeth. In North America many Indian tribes in the Southeast chewed the thick sap from a plant called Indian cup, or ragged cup. Early European colonists to the Americas learned from American Indians how to chew ragged cup sap to clean their teeth. The Choctaw of the Southeast also used a plant called button brush. The Gabrielino people of Southern California boiled milkweed sap to thicken it and then chewed it.

The Aztec used unsweetened chewing gum made from chicle to prevent tooth decay. Chicle is the milky latex of the tropical sapodilla tree, which is native to Mesoamerica.

The Aztec polished their teeth with charcoal, chilies, and salt. *(Library of Congress, Rare Books Division)*

▲▼▲▼▲▼▲▼▲▼▲▼▲▼▲▼▲▼▲▼▲▼▲▼▲▼▲▼▲

CHEWING GUM TO CLEAN TEETH

During 1998 special chewing gums were marketed in the United States as a breakthrough in dental care. These cavity-preventing gums were called chewable dentifrices. This "new" idea was really an old one. The American Indians chewed on substances to clean their teeth hundreds of years before contact with Europeans.

▼▲▼▲▼▲▼▲▼▲▼▲▼▲▼▲▼▲▼▲▼▲▼▲▼▲▼▲▼

Most bad breath, or halitosis, is caused by problems of the teeth and mouth. These include tooth decay, gum disease, and plaque on the back of the tongue. Bacteria cause all of these conditions. When the bacteria in the mouth break down food, they emit (give off) a gas. The odor of this gas is what people call bad breath.

American Indians of the Northeast chewed the sap from spruce trees. Spruce contains phytochemicals that work as antiseptics, which kill bacteria. American Indians taught New England colonists to chew spruce sap as a breath freshener. Spruce gum was sold by the lump in the eastern United States by the early 1800s.

Some Indian people chewed charcoal as a breath freshener. Charcoal is wood that has been burned so that all that remains is carbon. The chemical element carbon attracts the molecules of other carbon-based substances. These chemicals bond to the carbon, and they become trapped in the charcoal. Because carbon is a hard substance it removes plaque and food on teeth as well.

Aztec people chewed chicle, the sap from the sapodilla tree, to freshen their breath and keep their teeth clean. This picture shows a person getting ready to chew a piece of gum. *(Library of Congress, Rare Books Division)*

DENTAL TREATMENTS OF NORTH AMERICA

Even though American Indians took care of their teeth, sometimes they experienced tooth decay, gum disease, or sores in their mouths. The Indian people of the Americas had many ways of treating these problems. They used mouthwashes made from plants to treat gum disease and to heal sores in the mouth. They used other medicines to ease the pain of aching teeth. Gum disease, which is sometimes called periodontal disease, is an infection that is caused by bacteria. In time the bone beneath the gums can become infected. Eventually the bone cannot support the teeth, and they become loose and may even fall out. To tighten the gums so that they would better hold the teeth in place, the Costanoan people of California used a mouthwash that they made from the bark of the buckeye tree. This medicine also reduced pain. The Cherokee used the roots of a plant called ironweed to treat loose teeth.

Many Indian tribes in northeastern North America used tea that they made from the roots of the gold thread plant as a mouthwash. Gold thread contains a substance that relieves pain. American Indians who lived in the Great Lakes region rubbed gold thread tea on the gums of teething babies. They also used gold thread to treat thrush, a yeast infection of the mouth that is common in infants. Indians of the Northeast used gold thread as a canker sore cure. A canker sore is a small and painful sore in the mouth. Canker sores can be triggered by biting the inside of the cheek, vitamin deficiencies, food allergies, or viral infections. Gold thread was so effective that early colonists in North America, who learned about it from the Indian people, used it as a mouthwash as well.

To stop their teeth from aching, the Dakota, Lakota, and Nakota people of the Great Plains chewed on pieces of sweet flag

▲▽▲▽▲▽▲▽▲▽▲▽▲▽▲▽▲▽▲▽▲▽▲▽▲▽▲▽▲

TEMPORARY FILLINGS

Because decay eats away at the enamel of the teeth, eventually the nerves in the inner part of the teeth, or dentine, are exposed. Tooth pain is caused when air or food reaches these nerves. The Tewa people of the Southwest used the gum from the juniper bush as a filling for teeth that had cavities.

▼▲▽▲▽▲▽▲▽▲▽▲▽▲▽▲▽▲▽▲▽▲▽▲▽▲▽▲▽▼

roots. The Kootenai of the Plateau and the Anishinabe of the Northeast used the same treatment, as did the Cree of the Subarctic. Kootenai people also chewed on wild mint leaves to take away tooth pain. The Anishinabe dug lady's slipper root. Then they washed it and put it on painfully decayed teeth. Cherokee people used the poplar tree as a toothache remedy. The inner bark from this tree contains salicin, from which aspirin is made today.

When tooth pain was too intense to treat with plant medicines, Indians of North America removed decayed teeth. Sometimes they worked them loose and pulled them by hand. Usually they removed decayed teeth by striking them out with a tool carved from bone or antler. They made some tools for tooth removal from rock. For example, the Inuit people of the Arctic used a special tool to strike decayed teeth in order to remove them. They made it by inserting a blunt point of hard stone into a short wooden handle. They wrapped the handle with sinew to hold the blade in place. Sinew is the strong tissue that holds an animal's muscle to its bones.

DENTAL TREATMENTS OF MESOAMERICA

Aztec dentists were called *tlantonaniztli* in Nahuatl, the Aztec language. They developed standard prescriptions for preventing bad breath and tooth decay as well as gum disease. These ancient dentists had special names for each of the teeth. They instructed patients on the use of the toothpick to remove bits of food that had become stuck between the teeth. The Aztec called a toothpick a *netlantataconi*.

The Maya, whose culture arose about 1500 B.C. in Mesoamerica, discovered how to make dental inlays to repair teeth with cavities in

▲▼▲▼▲▼▲▼▲▼▲▼▲▼▲▼▲▼▲▼▲▼▲▼▲▼▲

REMOVING TARTAR

The Aztec visited a dentist when tartar built up on their teeth. The dentist scraped tartar from the teeth with a metal tool. Afterward, the dentist polished the patient's teeth. These dentists also pulled decayed teeth. When they had finished with the dental work, Aztec dentists made a salt-and-water mouth rinse that they told patients to use. Modern dentists instruct patients to rinse their mouths with salty water after having teeth pulled. Salty water cleans the mouth and reduces bacteria so that the mouth heals quickly.

▼▲▼▲▼▲▼▲▼▲▼▲▼▲▼▲▼▲▼▲▼▲▼▲▼▲▼

▲▽▲▽▲▽▲▽▲▽▲▽▲▽▲▽▲▽▲▽▲▽▲▽▲▽▲

DENTISTS' DRILLS

The first Maya dentists drilled teeth with a bow drill to make decorative holes or to clean and smooth a cavity made by decay. The drill bits that Maya dentists used were made of copper and were hollow. They were about an inch long. The dentist mounted the drill bit on a stick, or shaft. To turn the shaft, the dentist used a bow. A bow is a piece of string or sinew that is held taut by a curved piece of wood. This simple machine allowed the dentist to do more work with less effort than turning the shaft of the drill by hand.

▼▲▽▲▽▲▽▲▽▲▽▲▽▲▽▲▽▲▽▲▽▲▽▲▽▲▽

them. An inlay is a solid filling made to the exact shape of a tooth cavity and cemented into place. The Maya began filling teeth in about 1000 B.C.

Maya dentists used gold or semiprecious stones to make fillings for teeth. The stones they used included jade, hematite, and turquoise. They set these fillings into incisors and canines, the cutting teeth at the front of the mouth. Maya dentists also set inlays into premolars, the teeth right behind the canine teeth. They filled both lower and upper teeth.

Scientists who study the past believe that the Maya used fillings mainly to decorate teeth. Teeth set with semiprecious stones were fashionable among the upper class of ancient Maya society. Ancient Maya dentists also made fillings for teeth that had decayed.

Ancient Mesoamerican dentists knew that if they drilled too deeply into the tooth they would hit the pulp. A tooth's pulp is the soft center that contains nerves and blood vessels. A hole that was too deep could cause great pain and lead to an infection.

Maya dentists were so skilled that after more than 2,000 years the fillings that they made are still securely in Maya teeth. Archaeologists, scientists who study the past, are not sure of the type of glue that the Maya dentists used to keep the fillings from falling out. They believe that the Maya probably used copal glue for dental work.

The Maya made copal glue from the resin of the copal tree. A resin is a substance that will dissolve in alcohol or certain oils, but

Mayan Dentistry

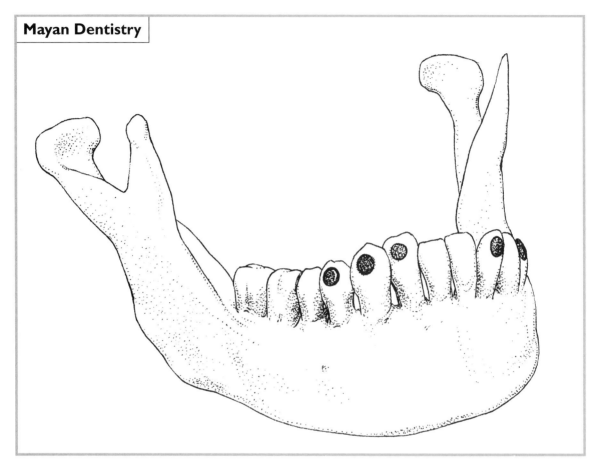

Maya dentists filled teeth with semiprecious stones in order to decorate them. They also were able to fill teeth that were decayed. *(© Facts On File)*

not in water. After the resin aged, it thickened (if copal is left undisturbed for several million years, it hardens into amber). Modern dentists throughout the world often use copal varnish to seal a tooth cavity after they remove the decay. The layer of copal sits between the tooth and the metal filling. It seals the tooth and insulates the nerve from heat and cold.

Medicine for the Mind and Body

American Indian healers looked at many parts of their patients' lives when they treated illnesses. They knew that thoughts, emotions, and beliefs could result in disease. American Indian healers used plant medicines and surgery to treat sick people, but they did not limit themselves to healing the symptoms of illness that the patient's body showed. For example, if a patient had broken a bone, an Indian healer might burn incense and pray when he or she was setting the bone back in place.

American Indian healers talked with their patients about what emotions they were feeling. They listened carefully to what their patients said in order to learn if their lives were out of balance or important needs were not being met. Modern mental health workers talk to their patients in much the same way. American Indian doctors involved a patient's family in treatment and made certain that the sick person's family was cared for. Today hospitals hire social workers for much the same purpose. Many American Indian doctors also used massage therapy and aromatherapy, two practices that are used by many non-Indians today.

American Indian healers also used songs, prayers, and ceremonies (formal gatherings) to help heal sick people. Today researchers are learning that belief and faith are important for wellness and for recovery from disease. Most modern hospitals have chaplains, religious workers who help patients meet spiritual needs. Many doctors and hospital programs help patients with life-threatening illnesses, such as cancer and AIDS, focus on these concerns in addition to treating the disease by giving patients drugs and performing surgery.

Today these ancient American Indian ways of healing are called complementary medical practices when they are used with medicine or surgery. They are called alternative medical practices when they are used instead of medicines or surgery. Many of them have become an accepted part of medical treatment.

THE MIND-BODY CONNECTION

Early European-trained physicians in the Americas often believed that American Indian healing ceremonies were crude magic that came from ignorance. They called American Indian healers witch doctors and made fun of many of their methods for treating patients. Only in the second half of the 20th century did modern scientists begin to fully understand the science that underlies these ancient American Indian ways of healing.

Today medical researchers know that emotions, feelings, and beliefs can affect the immune system in both positive and negative ways. When people feel fear or anger, their adrenal glands, which are located above the kidneys, produce large amounts of cortisol and epinephrine. Cortisol and epinephrine are hormones that cause the heart to beat faster and blood pressure to rise. Cortisol also releases glucose, or blood sugar, into the bloodstream. These hormones prepare the body to fight or run away. They also put the body's systems under a great deal of stress and weaken the immune system.

People who feel fearful or angry over long periods of time often develop stress-related illnesses. Some of these illnesses include heart attacks, strokes, headaches, stomach ulcers, and diabetes. People whose immune systems have been weakened by stress are more apt to catch contagious diseases, such as colds and flu. Their bodies are also less able to fight diseases such as cancer, AIDS, and rheumatoid arthritis. (Rheumatoid arthritis is a painful inflammation,

This portrait of the Sioux medicine man Fool Bull was taken in about 1900. While some medicine men of the plains healed sick people, others, like Fool Bull, were primarily war chiefs. *(J.A. Anderson, photographer/Library of Congress, Prints and Photographs Division [LC-USZ62-86441])*

After giving a sick person medicine, an American Indian healer of the Plains sings to the patient. This drawing was made in the mid-1800s by Seth Eastman. *(Courtesy of the National Library of Medicine)*

or swelling, of the joints that is caused when the body's own immune system attacks the lining of the joints.)

Modern medical researchers have found that just as stress can cause illnesses or make them worse, reducing stress can help keep people well. Relaxation (reducing stress) lowers blood pressure and slows the speed at which the heart beats. Calming thoughts and feelings boost the immune system's ability to fight disease.

PSYCHOTHERAPY

Because the mind influences the body, good mental health is very important for physical health. The Aztec, who established an empire in what is now Mexico in about A.D. 1100, and the Iroquois and Huron of the Northeast developed and practiced psychotherapy well before contact with Europeans. Other groups of American Indians used similar treatments for mental illnesses and physical problems that were caused by stress.

▲▼▲▼▲▼▲▼▲▼▲▼▲▼▲▼▲▼▲▼▲▼▲▼▲▼▲▼▲

AN ANCIENT PRACTICE

Psychotherapy is the treatment of mental or emotional problems, usually by talking with a professional. Today these professionals include counselors, social workers, psychologists, and psychiatrists. Although Sigmund Freud, a Viennese physician, is credited with inventing this technique in the 1890s, American Indians used similar techniques for hundreds of years before this time.

▼▲▼▲▼▲▼▲▼▲▼▲▼▲▼▲▼▲▼▲▼▲▼▲▼▲▼▲▼

Aztec physicians asked patients to talk about what they thought had caused the illness when other treatments failed to work or worked only for a short time. If a patient had done something wrong and was feeling guilty about it, an Aztec doctor might tell that person to bathe immediately. Bathing also stood for emotional cleansing. Aztec doctors might also suggest other ceremonies. These ceremonies allowed the patient to accept what he or she had done and move forward.

The Iroquois and Huron of North America also practiced psychotherapy. When plant medicines did not cure a patient's illness, the Iroquois and Huron believed that the disease was caused by feelings and needs that the sick person had not expressed. These emotions

▲▼▲▼▲▼▲▼▲▼▲▼▲▼▲▼▲▼▲▼▲▼▲▼▲▼▲▼▲▼▲

DEPRESSION

The Aztec recognized that depression was an illness. According to Aztec physicians, people who held public office were more apt to become depressed and overly tired than ordinary people. Modern doctors know that stress can trigger emotional illnesses such as depression and that feeling tired much of the time is a symptom of depression.

▼▲▼▲▼▲▼▲▼▲▼▲▼▲▼▲▼▲▼▲▼▲▼▲▼▲▼▲▼▲▼

THE HEALING POWER OF STORIES

Indian people of North America, many parts of Mesoamerica, and South America had oral cultures. They did not write information. Instead they told stories. Sometimes they sang their stories as songs. Many of these stories recalled the history of the tribe. Other stories taught children important lessons about how to live in balance with the Earth and as part of the tribal community. Patients told their dream stories to American Indian healers. These healers often told stories to their patients too.

Today many cognitive scientists, who study the mind, believe that human beings make sense of things that happen to them by telling stories. Making a story helps the person find meaning in their life experience. Telling a story and hearing a story connects the storyteller and the listener. Once their story is told and known, people with emotional problems can change that story to make a new one that helps them cope better. Modern psychologists who use storytelling to help clients are called narrative therapists.

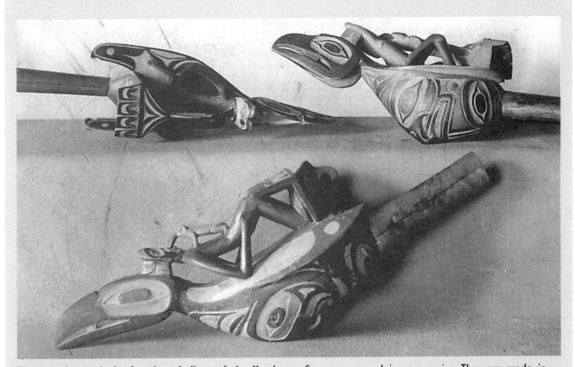

These rattles made by American Indians of the Northwest Coast were used in ceremonies. They are made in the shape of birds that were powerful symbols for the people who used them. *(Frank and Frances Carpenter Collection, Library of Congress, Prints and Photographs Division [Lot 11453-6, no 5])*

and wishes were often shown in dreams. If the soul's desires were not met, it became angry. This anger caused the person to become sick. When the soul had been satisfied, the person would recover. Modern psychologists call the part of the mind that hides memories and emotions from awareness the subconscious.

Huron and Iroquois healers asked their patients to talk about their dreams. Often people shared their dreams with the community. The healers helped explain to the patient what the dreams might mean. Then the healers told the patient what to do in order to make his or her soul happy again. Often the cure was a ceremony or feast that included the whole community.

A number of American Indian groups in addition to the Huron and Iroquois relied on dreams as important sources of information and guidance. Sometimes healers worked with dreams that had already happened. Often they advised a person to fast (go without food and water) and pray for a dream. Cherokee healers asked sick people many questions about their dreams in order to find the reason for their illness. These healers then told the dreamer what his or her dream meant and what to do to cure the illness. American Indians of the Northwest and the Inuit of the Arctic also interpreted dreams and used the information they contained for healing ceremonies. Indians of the Great Plains followed the guidance that they felt came to them in dreams. When people had bad dreams, North American Indian healers performed ceremonies to restore their peace of mind.

HEALING RELATIONSHIPS

American Indian people believed that illness affected the sick person's entire family. They knew that good relationships with family, friends, and the whole community were important to getting and staying healthy. Including the patient's family and the community in the treatment made it more likely to work. Family members and others in the community provided support for the sick person. Today research has shown that relationships are important for good health. Being surrounded by caring people increases a person's chances of living longer above that of people who are isolated.

Throughout the Americas, Indian people made certain that people with illnesses of the mind and body were well cared for. They made sure that everyone had food and a place to sleep. If the sick person's family was unable to take care of themselves, neighbors made sure that

Ceremonies involved families and entire villages in healing a person who was ill. This picture shows American Indians of the eastern part of what is now Canada taking part in a ceremony. The medicine man carries a turtle. This drawing was made in 1619. *(Library of Congress, Prints and Photographs Division [LC-USZ62-98770])*

they were well cared for too. If the patient died, people in the community continued to look after his or her family until they could meet their own needs. American Indians made certain that old people and those with disabilities had food and a place to live.

The people who helped the sick person and his or her family also gained health benefits. Modern researchers at Cornell University have found that people who volunteer to help other people feel better about themselves than do people who do not help others. Researchers at the University of Michigan have learned that people who spend time helping others tend to live longer than those who do not.

AROMATHERAPY

The idea that scents can affect mood and health is called aromatherapy. Indians of North American tribes burned dried Indian sage, sweetgrass, or cedar for purification, or cleansing, before they prayed. The Choctaw, a Plains tribe, used medicinal plants in their sweat lodges.

The Aztec believed that pleasant aromas were connected to the gods and that to smell these would brighten a person's mood and increase health. Aztec physicians had their patients smell the fragrances of certain flowers to relieve depression and tiredness. They even planted large gardens that were filled with fragrant flowers whose scents were valued for their healing effects.

Incense made from the gum of the copal tree was important to the Aztec. They believed it lessened the symptoms of epilepsy. Priests burned copal incense to purify both temples and houses of negative spiritual influences. The Aztec traded copal to the Maya, who called it *pom*. The Maya also used copal for purification and prayer.

Modern research shows that phytochemicals in plant medicines can enter the bloodstream through the lungs when smoke or strong scents are inhaled. Smelling certain scents has been shown to reduce anxiety (nervousness or mild fear), lower blood pressure, and help people with insomnia, a sleeping difficulty, get a good night's rest. When people associate a scent with a pleasant memory it can put them in a relaxed frame of mind.

CEREMONIES

Indian people throughout the Americas believed that many diseases were spiritually caused and needed a spiritual cure. Often that cure took the shape of a ceremony. American Indian ceremonies were

CHARLES ALEXANDER EASTMAN

Charles Alexander Eastman, a Santee Dakota Sioux, was the first American Indian physician to graduate from medical school. He was born in 1858 in Minnesota. As a boy he was raised in traditional ways and was given the Indian name Ohiyesa.

Eastman graduated from Boston University in 1890. He first worked as a doctor at the Pine Ridge Agency in South Dakota. After that he worked as a physician on several Indian reservations until 1903. Then he wrote several books about the American Indian way of life on the Great Plains. These include *Indian Boyhood, Old Indian Days,* and *The Soul of the Indian.* He also helped the Boy Scouts of America by lecturing on Indian culture and giving nature walks.

Charles Eastman worked hard to make certain that American Indians would obtain the rights they deserved. Eastman believed that Indian people did not have to give up their culture to succeed. Of the American Indian medicine man, he wrote, "However good his medicines might be—and undoubtedly some of them were efficacious—he never lost sight of the spiritual side of health and disease." He believed that when medicine men did ceremonies to drive evil spirits from sick people, they were treating depression. Charles Eastman died in 1939.

Charles Alexander Eastman, whose Indian name was Ohiyesa, was a doctor who fought for the rights of the Indian people. During his first job at the Pine Ridge Agency hospital in what is now South Dakota, he treated survivors of the Wounded Knee massacre. *(Library of Congress, Prints and Photographs Division [LC-USZ62-102275])*

These Indians of what is now Virginia are holding a ceremony on the bank of an ocean inlet. The fencelike structures in the background are fishing traps. This engraving by Theodore de Bry was first published in 1590. *(Library of Congress, Prints and Photographs Division [LC-USZ62-54017])*

made up of songs, dances, and prayers. Each Indian tribe used different ceremonies to treat illnesses. Within a tribe, each healer also had his or her own unique way of conducting ceremonies.

American Indian healers used many symbols in their ceremonies. A symbol is something that represents, or stands for, something else. For example, in a healing ceremony a dancer dressed like
a bad spirit might be a symbol of the sick person's disease. A dancer
dressed like a good spirit might stand for wellness. As the spirit of
wellness fought with and defeated the spirit of disease, the patient
would remember what it felt like to be well. The sick person could
also imagine a similar battle taking place in his or her body and
would see wellness winning.

The imagination has a powerful effect on the body. Modern
researchers have learned that when people visualize or imagine
something happening, their bodies react as if what they were seeing
in their mind's eye were real. When a person watches a scary movie,
the movie viewer knows that what is happening on the screen is not
real. Even so, his or her heart starts beating faster. If the movie is very
frightening, the person watching it may find his or her hands sweating and shaking. When the monster jumps out at the hero, many
people who are watching the movie jump and scream. Their minds
know the monster is a special effect, but their bodies react as if they
were in real danger. Imagining positive symbols and events can have
a relaxing effect on the body.

Starting in the 1970s some doctors experimented with having
patients visualize images as a way to treat disease. In the studies that
have been done so far, guided imagery (being coached to imagine
certain images unfold in the mind) has been found to decrease blood
sugar levels and heart rate. It also reduces anxiety and feelings of
pain. Some studies show that guided imagery helps people heal more
quickly from broken bones and cuts. It has also been shown to
shorten hospital stays. In three studies that were reported in 2002,
guided imagery boosted immune system function.

THE FUTURE OF AMERICAN INDIAN
MIND-BODY MEDICINE

The Indian Health Service, which provides medical care for Indian
people in the United States, works with American Indian healers to
make sure that traditional healing methods, as well as modern methods, are used in their hospitals. The interest in mind/body medicine
extends much further. Fifteen percent of all hospitals in the United
States offer some form of complementary medicine to their patients.

Two-thirds of all U.S. medical schools offer at least one class in complementary medicine.

Today the U.S. government funds research in many of the mind-body methods of healing that American Indians used for thousands of years. The National Center for Complementary and Alternative Medicine is part of the National Institutes of Health. Researchers who work there are studying treatments such as aromatherapy, massage, prayer, and art therapy in order to learn which ones can effectively treat illnesses.

GLOSSARY OF ANCIENT CULTURES OF THE AMERICAS

This glossary lists some of the important cultures, empires, and city-states in the Americas before 1492. Many of them existed hundreds or thousands of years before Europeans arrived in the Americas. Archaeologists try to piece together the history of America's ancient people from their buildings and the smaller objects they left behind. They can only make educated guesses based on the artifacts that they find.

The history of ancient America is one of changes. Because of this, modern people often mistakenly think that entire groups of ancient Indian people disappeared. Indian people and their civilizations did not vanish. Governments rose to power, fell, and were replaced by other governments. Sometimes large groups of people moved. They shared ideas with their neighbors and borrowed ideas from them. The Indians who made up civilizations of the past are the ancestors of the Indians of the Americas who are alive today.

Adena The Adena culture arose along the valleys of the Mississippi and Ohio Rivers and lasted from about 1500 B.C. to A.D. 200. Adena people were farmers and built burial mounds. The Hopewell people followed them.

Anasazi The Anasazi lived in the southwestern part of what is now the United States in New Mexico, Arizona, Utah, and Colorado. Their culture flourished from about 350 B.C. to

A.D. 1450. They are thought to be the ancestors of modern Pueblo people.

Aztec (Mexica)   The Aztec moved into the Valley of Mexico from the north in about A.D. 1100. Their culture followed that of the Toltec in the region. By 1350 they had expanded their empire and became the dominant state in what became central Mexico. They were the powerful group in that area when the Spaniards arrived. At its largest, the main Aztec city of Tenochtitlán had about 250,000 residents.

Chalchihuite   The Chalchihuite people entered what is now the Sierra Madre of Mexico between A.D. 900 and 1250. They were colonized by the Aztec after the Aztec Empire rose to power. They lived in what was considered the northern frontier of the Aztec Empire.

Chavin   Chavin culture flourished in the fertile river valleys of what is now Peru from about 1000 B.C. to about 200 B.C. The Chavin lived about 1,200 to 2,000 years before the Inca Empire was established.

Chimu   The Chimu civilization lasted from 1100 A.D. to the mid-1400s in what is now Peru. The Chimu state was conquered by the Inca.

Chinchorro   The Chinchorro culture, on the coast of what is now Peru, began in about 5000 B.C. It reached its peak in about 3000 B.C. The Chinchorro are best known for the elaborate ways in which they mummified their dead. They are one of the most ancient cultures to have lived in the region.

Hohokam   The Hohokam culture arose in what is now central and southern Arizona in about 300 B.C. Hohokam people are thought to be the ancestors of the Akimel O'odham (Pima) and the Tohono O'odham (Papago). The Hohokam lived in the Southwest in the same time period as the Anasazi. Their settlements were south of those of the Anasazi.

Hopewell   Hopewell culture arose along the valleys of the Mississippi and Ohio Rivers in about 300 B.C. The Hopewell are considered part of the Mound Builders, along with the Adena people who came before them. They built huge earthworks and flourished until about A.D. 700. They were followed by the Mississippian Culture.

Inca   The Inca established an empire in what is now Peru in about A.D. 1000 and rapidly expanded it. This empire extended from what is now northwest Argentina to parts of what is now Colombia. The Inca Empire was in power when the Spanish conquistador Francisco Pizarro arrived in South America.

Iroquois League (Haudenosaunee)   The Iroquois League, or Haudenosaunee, was an alliance of Northeast tribes established some time between A.D. 1000 and 1400. The tribes included the Oneida, Mohawk, Cayuga, Onondaga, Seneca, and later the Tuscarora.

Maya   The Maya civilization arose in what is now the Yucatán Peninsula of Mexico starting in about 1500 B.C. They did not have a centralized government but instead formed city-states. Maya people also lived in what are now Belize, Guatemala, El Salvador, and Honduras. When the Aztec expanded their empire, they began collecting taxes from the Maya and demanded loyalty to the Aztec Emperor.

Mississippian Culture   The Mississippian Culture arose in about A.D. 1000. Sometimes these people are called temple mound builders. Unlike the Adena and Hopewell people, they built earthworks for temples and ceremonial centers, rather than for burials. They built Cahokia, a city of about 30,000 people, near what is St. Louis, Missouri, today. Mississippian Culture started to weaken in the 1500s, but early French explorers encountered some temple mound builders in the late 1600s.

Mixtec   The Mixtec lived in what is now southern Mexico. Their culture arose in about A.D. 900. The Aztec Empire eventually dominated the Mixtec city-states, but their culture continued to thrive until the arrival of the Spaniards.

Moche   The Moche culture arose on the northern coast of what is now Peru in about 200 B.C. It flourished until about A.D. 600. The Moche were master artists.

Mound Builders   These were American Indians of several cultures who lived in the Mississippi and Ohio River Valleys over a period of time. Some Mound Builders also lived in the Southeast. These people of the Adena, Hopewell, and Mississippian cultures built extensive earthworks.

Nazca   The Nazca people lived in the lowlands of what is now Peru. Their culture arose starting in about 600 B.C. and lasted until about A.D. 900. Later the area where they lived became part of the Inca Empire.

Old Copper Culture   Peoples who lived from about 4000 B.C. to 1500 B.C. in the Great Lakes region of North America. These Indians worked with copper deposits that were close to the surface of the Earth. They made some of the earliest metal tools and objects in the world.

Olmec   The Olmec culture flourished starting in about 1700 B.C. in the coastal lowlands of what is now Mexico. It lasted until about 400 B.C. The Olmec built several cities, including La Venta, which had a population of about 18,000. The Olmec are also known as the Rubber People because they made items from rubber.

Paracas   The Paracas culture arose in the river valleys of what is now Peru in about 1300 B.C. and flourished until about A.D. 20. Paracas people invented many weaving and pottery techniques. A thousand years later, the area where they lived became part of the Inca Empire.

Paleo-Indians   A general term for those who lived before about 4000 B.C. They were the oldest peoples of the Americas. They hunted for their food, killing large mammals, such as the wooly mammoth and the mastodon.

Poverty Point Culture   The people of Poverty Point lived in the Lower Mississippi Valley between 1730 and 1350 B.C. They are a small, distinct group within Mississippian, or Mound Building, Culture.

Teotihuacán   The Teotihuacán culture flourished in the central valley of what is now Mexico from about 1000 B.C. to 900 A.D. At its center was the city-state of Teotihuacán, which was at its strongest from about A.D. 1 to about 650. In A.D. 500 the city was home to between 100,000 and 200,000 people.

Thule   The Thule culture arose in what is now northwestern Alaska between 1,000 and 2,000 years ago. Then it spread to Greenland. Thule people were the ancestors of the Inuit. They are known for their tool-making ability.

Toltec   The Toltec migrated into what is now known as the Valley of Mexico in central Mexico in about A.D. 800. They established their capital at Tula in about 900. About 60,000 people lived in Tula. The Toltec rule lasted until some time in the

1100s, when invading groups attacked and overthrew them. Little is known about the Toltec because the Aztec used the ruins of Tula as a source of building materials for their own monuments.

Zapotec   The Zapotec established a city-state south of the Mixtec in what is now southern Mexico. In about 500 B.C. they began building the city of Monte Albán. By A.D. 450, more than 15,000 people lived in Monte Albán. Later this grew to 25,000 people. By about 700 A.D. the Zapotec began moving away from their city. Although their culture remained, the Zapotec no longer had a city-state.

TRIBES ORGANIZED BY CULTURE AREA

North American Culture Areas

ARCTIC CULTURE AREA
Aleut
Inuit

CALIFORNIA CULTURE AREA
Achomawi (Pit River)
Akwaala
Alliklik (Tataviam)
Atsugewi (Pit River)
Bear River
Cahto (Kato)
Cahuilla
Chilula
Chimariko
Chumash
Costanoan (Ohlone)
Cupeño
Diegueño (Ipai)
Esselen
Fernandeño
Gabrieliño
Huchnom
Hupa
Ipai (Diegueño)
Juaneño
Kamia (Tipai)
Karok
Kitanemuk

Konomihu
Lassik
Luiseño
Maidu
Mattole
Miwok
Nicoleño
Nomlaki
Nongatl
Okwanuchu
Patwin (subgroup of Wintun)
Pomo
Salinas
Serrano
Shasta
Sinkyone
Tolowa (Smith River)
Tubatulabal (Kern River)
Vanyume
Wailaki
Wappo
Whilkut
Wintu (subgroup of Wintun)
Wintun
Wiyot
Yahi

Yana
Yokuts
Yuki
Yurok

GREAT BASIN CULTURE AREA
Bannock
Chemehuevi
Kawaiisu
Mono
Paiute
Panamint
Sheepeater (subgroup
of Bannock
and Shoshone)
Shoshone
Snake (subgroup of Paiute)
Ute
Washoe

GREAT PLAINS CULTURE AREA
Arapaho
Arikara
Assiniboine
Atsina (Gros Ventre)
Blackfeet
Blood (subgroup of Blackfeet)
Cheyenne
Comanche
Crow
Hidatsa
Ioway
Kaw
Kichai
Kiowa
Kiowa-Apache
Mandan
Missouria
Omaha
Osage
Otoe
Pawnee
Piegan (subgroup of Blackfeet)

Plains Cree
Plains Ojibway
Ponca
Quapaw
Sarcee
Sioux (Dakota, Lakota, Nakota)
Tawakoni
Tawehash
Tonkawa
Waco
Wichita
Yscani

NORTHEAST CULTURE AREA
Abenaki
Algonkin
Amikwa (Otter)
Cayuga
Chippewa (Ojibway,
Anishinabe)
Chowanoc
Conoy
Coree (Coranine)
Erie
Fox (Mesquaki)
Hatteras
Honniasont
Huron (Wyandot)
Illinois
Iroquois (Haudenosaunee)
Kickapoo
Kitchigami
Lenni Lenape (Delaware)
Machapunga
Mahican
Maliseet
Manhattan (subgroup of Lenni
Lenape or Wappinger)
Massachuset
Mattabesac
Meherrin
Menominee
Miami

Micmac
Mingo (subgroup of Iroquois)
Mohawk
Mohegan
Montauk
Moratok
Nanticoke
Narragansett
Nauset
Neusiok
Neutral (Attiwandaronk)
Niantic
Nipmuc
Noquet
Nottaway
Oneida
Onondaga
Ottawa
Otter (Amikwa)
Pamlico (Pomeiok)
Passamaquoddy
Paugussett
Penacook
Penobscot
Pequot
Pocomtuc
Poospatuck
(subgroup of Montauk)
Potawatomi
Powhatan
Raritan
(subgroup of Lenni Lenape)
Roanoke
Sac
Sakonnet
Secotan
Seneca
Shawnee
Shinnecock
(subgroup of Montauk)
Susquehannock
Tobacco (Petun)

Tuscarora
Wampanoag
Wappinger
Weapemeoc
Wenro
Winnebago (Ho-Chunk)

**NORTHWEST COAST
CULTURE AREA**
Ahantchuyuk
Alsea
Atfalati
Bella Coola
Cathlamet
Cathlapotle
Chastacosta
Chehalis
Chelamela
Chepenafa (Mary's River)
Chetco
Chilluckittequaw
Chimakum
Chinook
Clackamas
Clallam
Clatskanie
Clatsop
Clowwewalla
Comox
Coos
Coquille (Mishikhwutmetunne)
Cowichan
Cowlitz
Dakubetede
Duwamish
Gitskan
Haida
Haisla
Heiltsuk
Kalapuya
Kuitsh
Kwakiutl

Kwalhioqua
Latgawa
Luckiamute
Lumni
Makah
Miluk
Muckleshoot
Multomah (Wappato)
Nanaimo
Nisga
Nisqually
Nooksack
Nootka
Puntlatch
Puyallup
Quaitso (Queets)
Quileute
Quinault
Rogue
Sahehwamish
Samish
Santiam
Seechelt
Semiahmoo
Siletz
Siuslaw
Skagit
Skilloot
Skykomish
Snohomish
Snoqualmie
Songish
Squamish
Squaxon (Squaxin)
Stalo
Swallah
Swinomish
Takelma (Rogue)
Taltushtuntude
Tillamook
Tlingit
Tsimshian

Tututni (Rogue)
Twana
Umpqua
Wappato (Multomah)
Wasco
Watlala (Cascade)
Yamel
Yaquina
Yoncalla

PLATEAU CULTURE AREA

Cayuse
Chelan
Coeur d'Alene
Columbia (Sinkiuse)
Colville
Entiat
Flathead (Salish)
Kalispel
Klamath
Klickitat
Kootenai (Flathead)
Lake (Senijextee)
Lillooet
Methow
Modoc
Molalla
Nez Perce
Ntlakyapamuk (Thompson)
Okanagan
Palouse
Pshwanwapam
Sanpoil
Shuswap
Sinkaietk
Sinkakaius
Skin (Tapanash)
Spokan
Stuwihamuk
Taidnapam
Tenino
Tyigh

Umatilla
Walla Walla
Wanapam
Wauyukma
Wenatchee
Wishram
Yakama

SOUTHEAST CULTURE AREA

Acolapissa
Adai
Ais
Akokisa
Alabama
Amacano
Apalachee
Apalachicola
Atakapa
Avoyel
Bayogoula
Bidai
Biloxi
Caddo
Calusa
Caparaz
Cape Fear
Catawba
Chakchiuma
Chatot
Chawasha (subgroup
of Chitimacha)
Cheraw (Sara)
Cherokee
Chiaha
Chickasaw
Chine
Chitimacha
Choctaw
Congaree
Coushatta
Creek
Cusabo
Deadose

Eno
Eyeish (Ayish)
Griga
Guacata
Guale
Hitchiti
Houma
Ibitoupa
Jeaga
Kaskinampo
Keyauwee
Koroa
Lumbee
Manahoac
Miccosukee
(subgroup of Seminole)
Mobile
Monacan
Moneton
Muklasa
Nahyssan
Napochi
Natchez
Occaneechi
Oconee
Ofo
Okelousa
Okmulgee
Opelousa
Osochi
Pasacagoula
Patiri
Pawokti
Pee Dee
Pensacola
Quinipissa
Santee (Issati)
Saponi
Sawokli
Seminole
Sewee
Shakori
Sissipahaw

Sugeree
Taensa
Tamathli
Tangipahoa
Taposa
Tawasa
Tekesta
Timucua
Tiou
Tohome
Tunica
Tuskegee
Tutelo
Waccamaw
Washa (subgroup of
  Chitimacha)
Wateree
Waxhaw
Winyaw
Woccon
Yadkin
Yamasee
Yazoo
Yuchi

SOUTHWEST CULTURE AREA
Akimel O'odham (Pima)
Apache
Coahuiltec
Cocopah
Halchidhoma
Halyikwamai
Havasupai
Hopi
Hualapai
Jumano (Shuman)
Karankawa
Keres (Pueblo Indians)
Kohuana
Maricopa
Mojave
Navajo (Dineh)
Piro (Pueblo Indians)

Pueblo
Quenchan (Yuma)
Shuman (Jumano)
Sobaipuri
Tewa (Pueblo Indians)
Tiwa (Pueblo Indians)
Tohono O'odham (Papago)
Towa (Jemez, Pueblo Indians)
Yaqui
Yavapai
Yuma (Quechan)
Zuni

SUBARCTIC CULTURE AREA
Ahtena (Copper)
Beaver (Tsattine)
Beothuk
Carrier
Chilcotin
Chipewyan
Cree
Dogrib
Eyak
Han
Hare (Kawchottine)
Ingalik
Kolchan
Koyukon
Kutchin
Montagnais
Nabesna
Nahane
Naskapi
Sekani
Slave (Slavery,
  Etchaottine)
Tahltan
Tanaina
Tanana
Tatsanottine (Yellowknife)
Tsetsaut
Tutchone (Mountain)

Mesoamerican Culture Area*

Aztec (Mexica-Nahuatl)   Olmec
Chalchiuites   Toltec
Maya   Zapotec
Mixtec

Circum-Caribbean Culture Area
(West Indies and Portion of Central America)

Arawak   Matagalpa
Boruca   Mosquito
Carib   Paya
Ciboney   Rama
Ciguayo   Silam
Coiba   Sumo
Corobici   Taino
Cuna   Talamanca
Guaymi   Ulva
Guetar   Voto
Jicaque   Yosco
Lucayo

South American Culture Areas*

ANDEAN CULTURE AREA   **CENTRAL AND**
Achuari   **SOUTHERN CULTURE AREA**
Aguaruna   Guarani
Chavin   Mapuche
Chimu
Inca   **TROPICAL FOREST (AMAZON**
Jivaro   **BASIN) CULTURE AREA**
Mapuche   Arawak
Moche   Carib
Nazca   Tupi
Quecha

* These lists do not attempt to include all groups in the area. They do, however, include a mix of ancient and modern peoples.

Appendix
MAPS

1. North American, Mesoamerican, and Circum-Caribbean Indian Culture Areas
2. Arctic Culture Area
3. Subarctic Culture Area
4. Northeast Culture Area
5. Southeast Culture Area
6. Great Plains Culture Area
7. Plateau Culture Area
8. Great Basin Culture Area
9. Northwest Coast Culture Area
10. California Culture Area
11. Southwest Culture Area
12. Mesoamerican Culture Area
13. Circum-Caribbean Culture Area
14. South American Culture Areas
15. Ancient Civilizations in the Americas, 1492

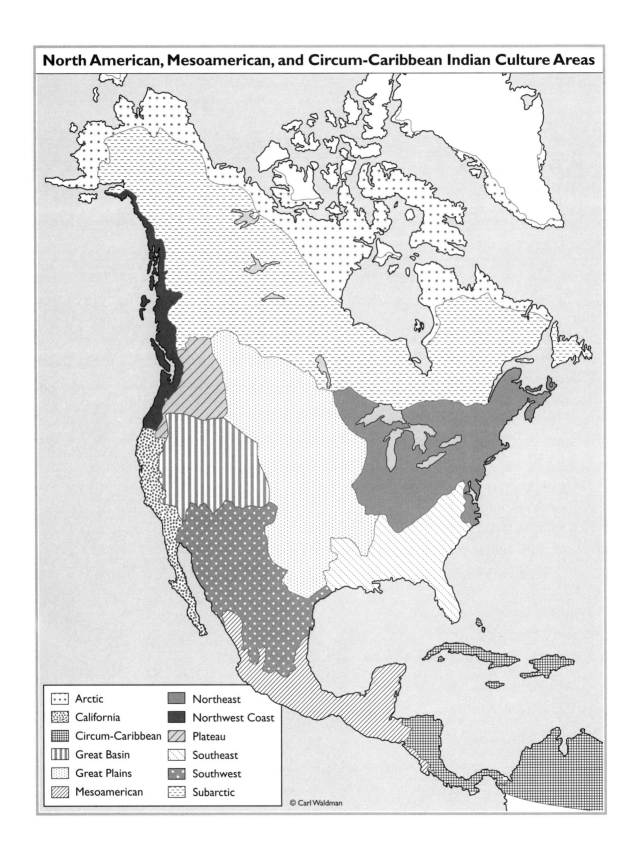

North American, Mesoamerican, and Circum-Caribbean Indian Culture Areas

Arctic

California

Circum-Caribbean

Great Basin

Great Plains

Mesoamerican

Northeast

Northwest Coast

Plateau

Southeast

Southwest

Subarctic

© Carl Waldman

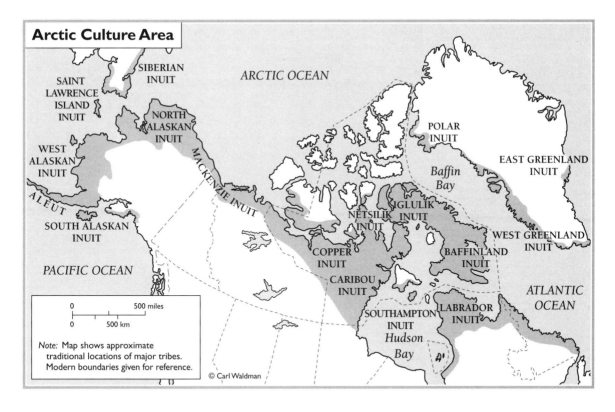

Arctic Culture Area

SAINT
LAWRENCE
ISLAND
INUIT

SIBERIAN
INUIT

ARCTIC OCEAN

WEST
ALASKAN
INUIT

NORTH
ALASKAN
INUIT

POLAR
INUIT

*Baffin
Bay*

EAST GREENLAND
INUIT

ALEUT

SOUTH ALASKAN
INUIT

MACKENZIE INUIT

NETSILIK
INUIT

IGLULIK
INUIT

WEST GREENLAND
INUIT

PACIFIC OCEAN

COPPER
INUIT

BAFFINLAND
INUIT

CARIBOU
INUIT

LABRADOR
INUIT

*ATLANTIC
OCEAN*

SOUTHAMPTON
INUIT
*Hudson
Bay*

0 — 500 miles
0 — 500 km

Note: Map shows approximate
traditional locations of major tribes.
Modern boundaries given for reference.

© Carl Waldman

Subarctic Culture Area

KOYUKON

*ARCTIC
OCEAN*

INGALIK

TANANA

TANAINA

KUTCHIN

HAN

HARE

NABESNA
AHTENA

TUTCHONE

TAGISH

TATSANOTTINE

TAHLTAN

NAHANE

DOGRIB

TSETSAUT

SLAVE

CHIPEWYAN

SEKANI

*Hudson
Bay*

CARRIER

BEAVER

NASKAPI

THOMPSON

CHILCOTIN

WESTERN
WOODS
CREE

*PACIFIC
OCEAN*

SWAMPY
CREE

WEST
MAIN
CREE

EAST MAIN
CREE

BEOTHUK

MONTAGNAIS

CHIPPEWA

ALGONKIN

TÊTE DE
BOULE
CREE

*ATLANTIC
OCEAN*

0 — 500 miles
0 — 500 km

Note: Map shows approximate
traditional locations of major tribes.
Modern boundaries given for reference.

© Carl Waldman

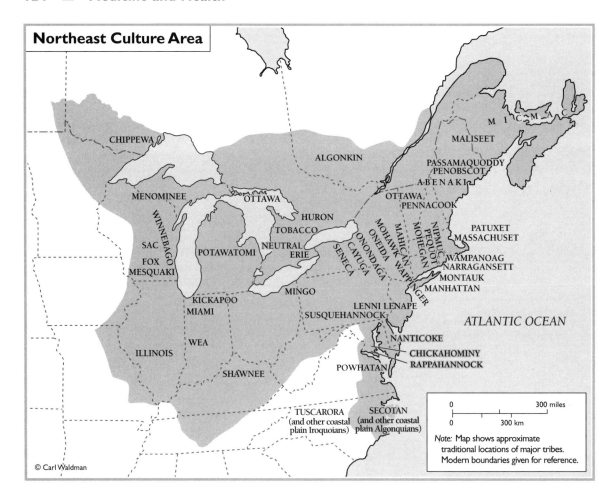

Northeast Culture Area

CHIPPEWA

ALGONKIN

MI C MA C

MALISEET

PASSAMAQUODDY
PENOBSCOT
ABENAKI

MENOMINEE   OTTAWA

OTTAWA
PENNACOOK

WINNEBAGO

SAC

FOX
MESQUAKI

POTAWATOMI

HURON

TOBACCO

NEUTRAL
ERIE

SENECA

CAYUGA

ONONDAGA

ONEIDA

MOHAWK

MAHICAN

WAPPINGER

MOHEGAN

PEQUOT

NIPMUC

PATUXET
MASSACHUSET

WAMPANOAG
NARRAGANSETT

MONTAUK

MANHATTAN

MINGO

KICKAPOO
MIAMI

LENNI LENAPE

SUSQUEHANNOCK

ATLANTIC OCEAN

WEA

ILLINOIS

NANTICOKE

CHICKAHOMINY
RAPPAHANNOCK

SHAWNEE

POWHATAN

TUSCARORA
(and other coastal
plain Iroquoians)

SECOTAN
(and other coastal
plain Algonquians)

0   300 miles

0   300 km

Note: Map shows approximate
traditional locations of major tribes.
Modern boundaries given for reference.

© Carl Waldman

Southeast Culture Area

SAPONI
MONACAN
TUTELO
ENO
YUCHI
SUGEREE WOCCON
CHEROKEE
CHICKASAW
CHERAW
CATAWBA
WATEREE
WACCAMAW
COUSHATTA
PEE DEE
SANTEE
TUSKEGEE
TAPOSA
CUSABO
CHAKCHIUMA
CADDO
NAPOCHI
CREEK (MUSKOGEE)
MIKASUKI
ALABAMA
HITCHITI
TUNICA
OFO
CHIAHA
YAZOO
YAMASEE
TAENSA
CHOCTAW
TOHOME
TAMATHLI (GUALE)
ATLANTIC OCEAN
NATCHEZ
CHATOT
HOUMA
BIDAI
MOBILE
OSOCHI
BILOXI
APALACHEE
ATAKAPA
PENSACOLA
CHITIMACHA
TIMUCUA
AIS
0   200 miles
SEMINOLE (19th century)
0   200 km
Gulf of Mexico
CALUSA
TEKESTA
Note: Map shows approximate
traditional locations of major tribes.
Modern boundaries given for reference.
© Carl Waldman

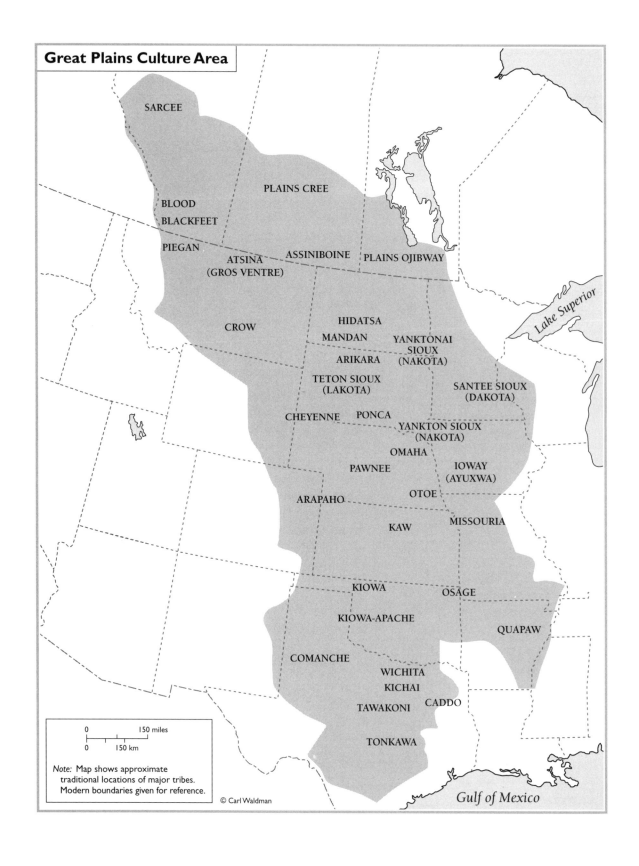

Great Plains Culture Area

SARCEE

PLAINS CREE

BLOOD
BLACKFEET
PIEGAN

ATSINA
(GROS VENTRE)

ASSINIBOINE   PLAINS OJIBWAY

CROW

HIDATSA
MANDAN   YANKTONAI
                    SIOUX
ARIKARA   (NAKOTA)

TETON SIOUX
(LAKOTA)   SANTEE SIOUX
                             (DAKOTA)

CHEYENNE   PONCA
                   YANKTON SIOUX
                   (NAKOTA)

OMAHA
PAWNEE   IOWAY
                       (AYUXWA)

ARAPAHO   OTOE

KAW   MISSOURIA

KIOWA   OSAGE

KIOWA-APACHE   QUAPAW

COMANCHE

WICHITA
KICHAI
              CADDO
TAWAKONI

TONKAWA

Lake Superior

Gulf of Mexico

0   150 miles
0   150 km

Note: Map shows approximate
traditional locations of major tribes.
Modern boundaries given for reference.

© Carl Waldman

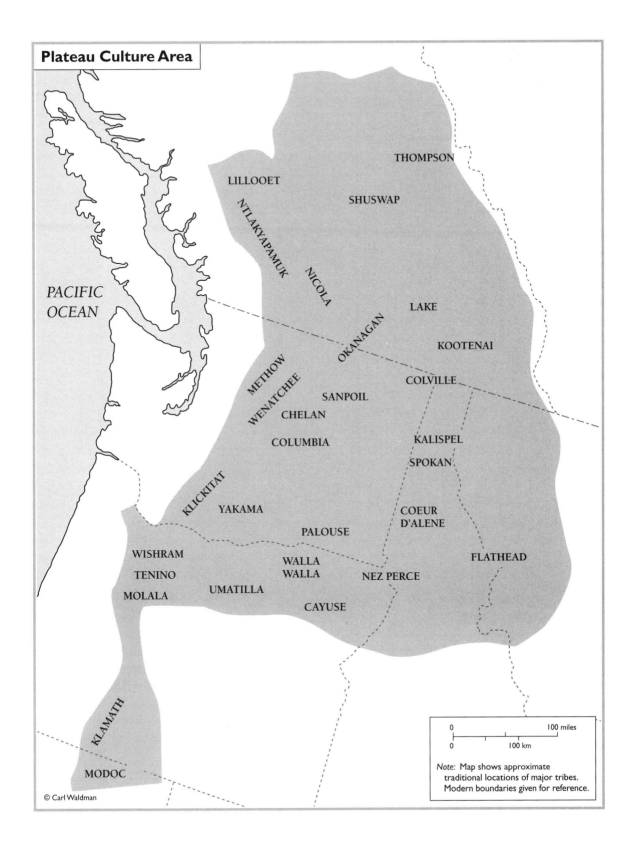

Plateau Culture Area

PACIFIC
OCEAN

THOMPSON

LILLOOET

NTLAKYAPAMUK

SHUSWAP

NICOLA

LAKE

OKANAGAN

KOOTENAI

METHOW

COLVILLE

WENATCHEE

SANPOIL

CHELAN

COLUMBIA

KALISPEL

SPOKAN

KLICKITAT

YAKAMA

COEUR
D'ALENE

PALOUSE

FLATHEAD

WISHRAM

WALLA
WALLA

TENINO

NEZ PERCE

MOLALA

UMATILLA

CAYUSE

KLAMATH

MODOC

© Carl Waldman

0   100 miles

0   100 km

Note: Map shows approximate
traditional locations of major tribes.
Modern boundaries given for reference.

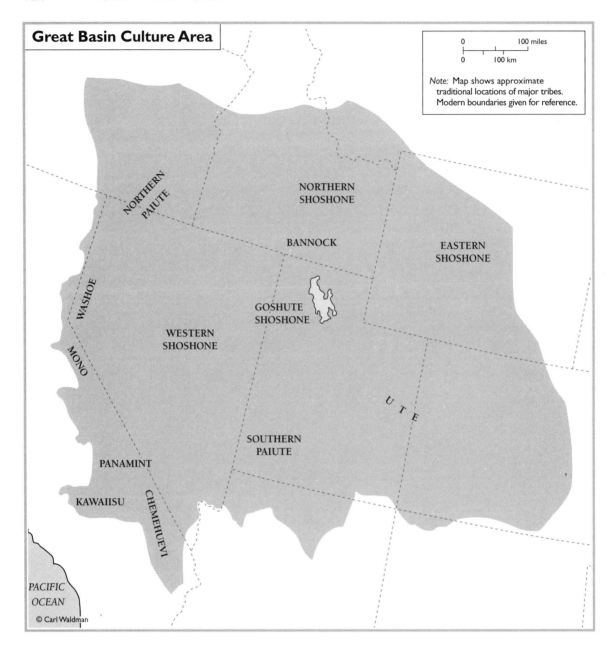

Great Basin Culture Area

0   100 miles
0   100 km

Note: Map shows approximate traditional locations of major tribes. Modern boundaries given for reference.

NORTHERN PAIUTE

NORTHERN SHOSHONE

BANNOCK

EASTERN SHOSHONE

WASHOE

GOSHUTE SHOSHONE

WESTERN SHOSHONE

MONO

U T E

SOUTHERN PAIUTE

PANAMINT

KAWAIISU

CHEMEHUEVI

PACIFIC OCEAN

© Carl Waldman

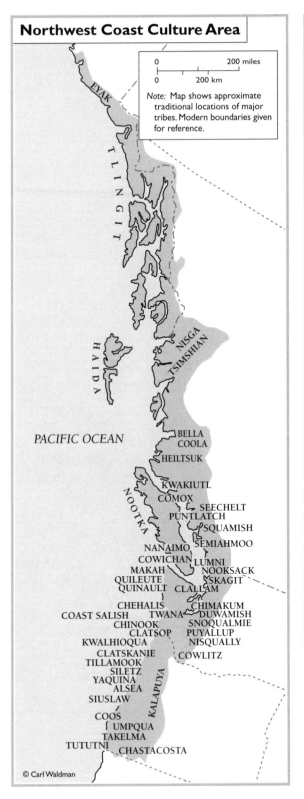

Northwest Coast Culture Area

0   200 miles
0   200 km

Note: Map shows approximate traditional locations of major tribes. Modern boundaries given for reference.

EYAK

TLINGIT

HAIDA

NISGA

TSIMSHIAN

PACIFIC OCEAN

BELLA COOLA

HEILTSUK

KWAKIUTL

COMOX

NOOTKA

SEECHELT

PUNTLATCH

SQUAMISH

SEMIAHMOO

NANAIMO

COWICHAN

LUMNI

MAKAH

NOOKSACK

QUILEUTE

SKAGIT

QUINAULT

CLALLAM

CHEHALIS

CHIMAKUM

COAST SALISH

TWANA

DUWAMISH

CHINOOK

SNOQUALMIE

CLATSOP

PUYALLUP

KWALHIOQUA

NISQUALLY

CLATSKANIE

COWLITZ

TILLAMOOK

SILETZ

YAQUINA

ALSEA

SIUSLAW

KALAPUYA

COOS

UMPQUA

TAKELMA

TUTUTNI

CHASTACOSTA

© Carl Waldman

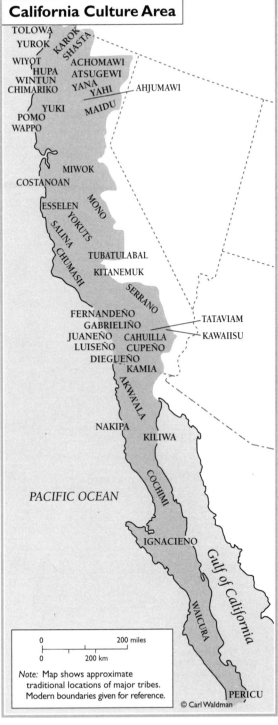

California Culture Area

TOLOWA

YUROK

KAROK

SHASTA

WIYOT

HUPA

ACHOMAWI

WINTUN

ATSUGEWI

CHIMARIKO

YANA

YAHI

AHJUMAWI

YUKI

POMO

MAIDU

WAPPO

MIWOK

COSTANOAN

ESSELEN

MONO

YOKUTS

SALINA

TUBATULABAL

CHUMASH

KITANEMUK

SERRANO

FERNANDEÑO

GABRIELIÑO

TATAVIAM

JUANEÑO

CAHUILLA

KAWAIISU

LUISEÑO

CUPEÑO

DIEGUEÑO

KAMIA

AKWAALA

NAKIPA

KILIWA

PACIFIC OCEAN

COCHIMI

Gulf of California

IGNACIENO

WAICURA

0   200 miles
0   200 km

Note: Map shows approximate traditional locations of major tribes. Modern boundaries given for reference.

PERICU

© Carl Waldman

Southwest Culture Area

HUALAPAI

HAVASUPAI

HOPI

MOJAVE

NAVAJO

JICARILLA
APACHE

HALCHIDHOMA

YAVAPAI

MARICOPA

ZUNI

TIWA

TOWA TEWA

PECOS

KERES

YUMA

COCOPAH

WESTERN
APACHE

PIRO

TIWA

TOHONO
O'ODHAM

MIMBRENO
APACHE

CHIRICAHUA
APACHE

MESCALERO
APACHE

AKIMEL
O'ODHAM

SUMA

OPATA

JUMANO

SERI

CAHITA

JOVA

CONCHO

YAQUI

TEPAHUE

TARAHUMARA

LIPAN
APACHE

VAVROHIO

MAYO

TOBOSO

KARANKAWA

ZOE

COMANITO

NIO

COAHUILTEC

LAGUNERO

GUASAVE

TEPEHUAN

ZACATEC

BOCALOS

JANAMBRE

PISONES

NEGRITO

TAMAULIPEC

*Gulf
of
Mexico*

HUICHOL

TEPECANO

COLOTLAN

TEUL

GUACHICHIL

GUAMARES

JONAZ

PAME

Gulf of California

PACIFIC OCEAN

0 ——— 150 miles

0 ——— 150 km

Note: Map shows approximate
traditional locations of major tribes.
Modern boundaries given for reference.

© Carl Waldman

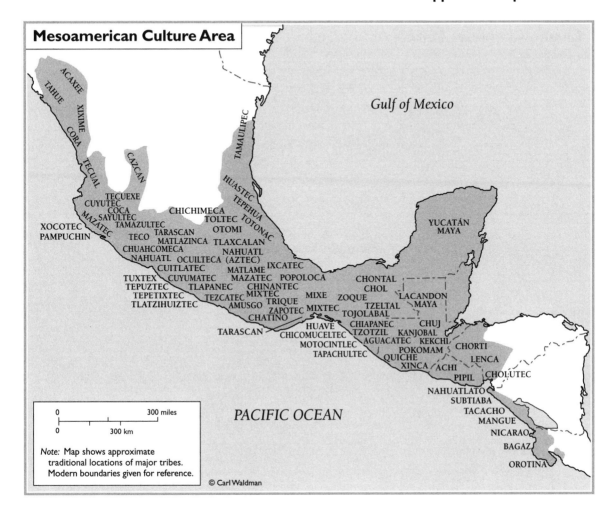

Mesoamerican Culture Area

Gulf of Mexico

ACAXEE
TAHUE
XIXIME
CORA
TECUAL
CAZCAN
TAMAULIPEC

HUASTEC
TEPEHUA
TOTONAC

TECUEXE
CUYUTEC
COCA
SAYULTEC
CHICHIMECA
TOLTEC
MAZATEC
TAMAZULTEC
OTOMI
XOCOTEC
TARASCAN
PAMPUCHIN
TECO
MATLAZINCA
TLAXCALAN
CHUAHCOMECA
NAHUATL
NAHUATL
OCUILTECA (AZTEC)
IXCATEC
CUITLATEC
MATLAME
TUXTEX
CUYUMATEC
MAZATEC
POPOLOCA
TEPUZTEC
TLAPANEC
CHINANTEC
TEPETIXTEC
MIXTEC
TEZCATEC
MIXE
TLATZIHUIZTEC
AMUSGO
TRIQUE
MIXTEC
ZAPOTEC
CHATINO
HUAVE
TARASCAN
CHICOMUCELTEC
MOTOCINTLEC
TAPACHULTEC

YUCATÁN
MAYA

CHONTAL
CHOL
ZOQUE
LACANDON
TZELTAL
MAYA
TOJOLABAL
CHIAPANEC
CHUJ
TZOTZIL
KANJOBAL
AGUACATEC
KEKCHI
POKOMAM
CHORTI
QUICHE
LENCA
XINCA
ACHI
PIPIL
CHOLUTEC
NAHUATLATO
SUBTIABA
TACACHO
MANGUE
NICARAO
BAGAZ
OROTINA

PACIFIC OCEAN

0 — 300 miles
0 — 300 km

Note: Map shows approximate
traditional locations of major tribes.
Modern boundaries given for reference.

© Carl Waldman

Circum-Caribbean Culture Area

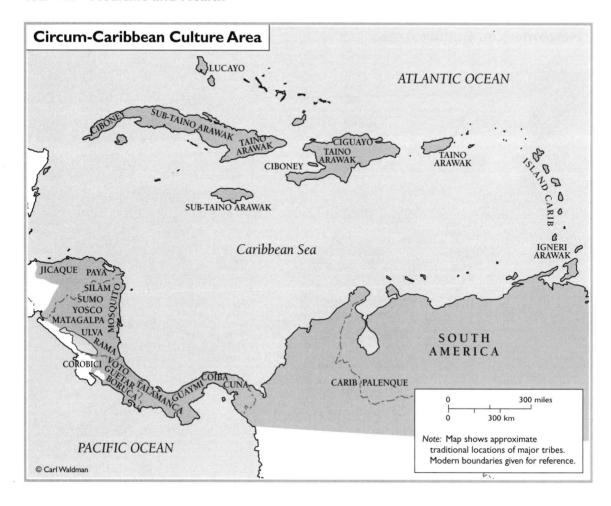

© Carl Waldman

South American Culture Areas

CIRCUM-CARIBBEAN

CARIB
PALENQUE

TUPI
ARAWAK

AGUARUNA
ACHUARI
JIVARO

CARIB

ARAWAK

TUPI

CHIMU

INCA

TROPICAL FOREST

ANDEAN

EASTERN
HIGHLANDS

GUARANI

GUARANI

CENTRAL AND SOUTHERN

MAPUCHE

PAMPAS

TIERRA DEL FUEGO

ANDEAN	Culture areas
PAMPAS	Regions
MAPUCHE	Tribes and peoples
————	Approximate culture area boundaries
··········	Approximate regional boundaries

0   800 miles
0   800 km

Note: See the Circum-Caribbean map for the entire scope of the culture area.

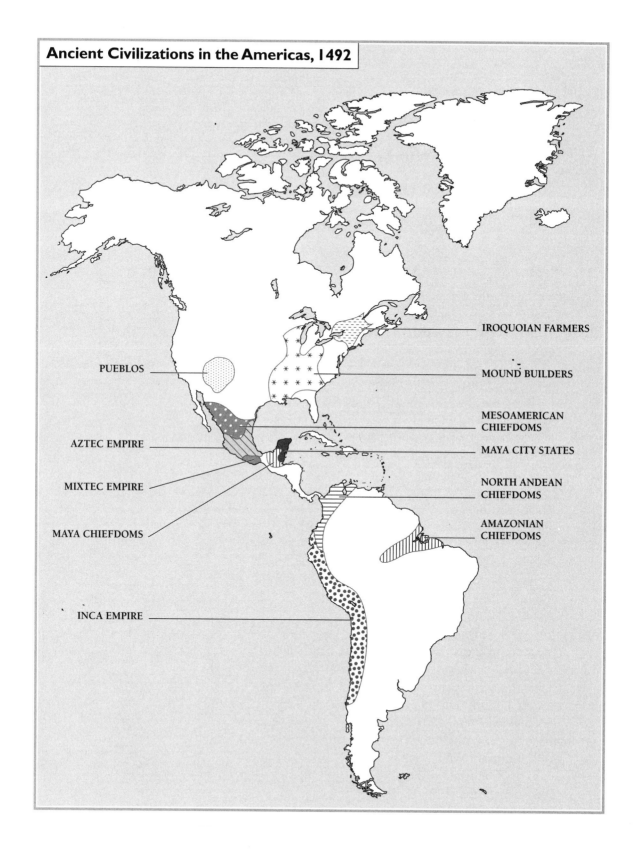

Ancient Civilizations in the Americas, 1492

IROQUOIAN FARMERS

PUEBLOS

MOUND BUILDERS

MESOAMERICAN
CHIEFDOMS

AZTEC EMPIRE

MAYA CITY STATES

MIXTEC EMPIRE

NORTH ANDEAN
CHIEFDOMS

MAYA CHIEFDOMS

AMAZONIAN
CHIEFDOMS

INCA EMPIRE

FURTHER READING

Baquedano, Elizabeth. *Aztec, Inca and Maya*. New York: DK Publishing, 2000.

Carrasco, David. *Daily Life of the Aztecs: Keepers of the Sun and Moon.* Westport, Conn.: Greenwood Press, 1998.

Densmore, Frances. *How Indians Use Wild Plants for Food, Medicine, and Crafts*. Mineola, N.Y.: Dover Publications, 1974.

Goodchild, Peter. *Survival Skills of the North American Indians*. 2d ed. Chicago: Chicago Review Press, 1999.

Hawke, Sharryl Davis, and James E. Davis. *Seeds of Change: The Story of Cultural Exchange after 1492*. New York: Addison-Wesley, 1993.

Johnson, Sylvia S. *Tomatoes, Potatoes, Corn & Beans: How Foods of the Americas Changed Eating around the World*. New York: Atheneum, 1997.

Keoke, Emory, and Kay Marie Porterfield. *The Encyclopedia of American Indian Contributions to the World: 15,000 Years of Inventions and Innovation*. New York: Facts On File, 2002.

Liptak, Karen. *North American Indian Survival Skills*. New York: Franklin Watts, 1990.

Malpass, Michael A. *Daily Life in the Inca Empire*. Westport, Conn.: Greenwood Press, 2002.

Murdoch, David. *Eyewitness: North American Indians*. New York: DK Publishers, 2000.

Sharer, Robert J. *Daily Life in Maya Civilization*. Westport, Conn.: Greenwood Press, 2002.

Steedman, Scott. *How Would You Survive As an American Indian?* New York: Franklin Watts, 1997.

Vogel, Virgil J. *American Indian Medicine*. Norman: University of Oklahoma Press, 1990.

Weiner, Michael A. *Earth Medicine, Earth Food: The Classic Guide to the Herbal Remedies and Wild Plants of the North American Indians.* New York: Fawcett Columbine, 1991.

Wood, Marian. *Ancient America: Cultural Atlas for Young People.* New York: Facts On File, 1990.

INDEX

Page numbers in *italic* indicate photographs. Page numbers in **boldface** indicate box features. Page numbers followed by *m* indicate maps. Page numbers followed by *g* indicate glossary entries. Page numbers followed by *t* indicate time line entries.